Military Draft

Other Books of Related Interest:

Opposing Viewpoints Series

The War on Terrorism

Current Controversies Series

America's Battle Against Terrorism

War

At Issue Series

Can the War on Terrorism Be Won?

Military Recruiters

"Congress shall make no law . . . abridging the freedom of speech, or of the press."

First Amendment to the U.S. Constitution

The basic foundation of our democracy is the First Amendment guarantee of freedom of expression. The Opposing Viewpoints Series is dedicated to the concept of this basic freedom and the idea that it is more important to practice it than to enshrine it.

Military Draft

Viqi Wagner, Book Editor

GREENHAVEN PRESS
A part of Gale, Cengage Learning

Detroit • New York • San Francisco • New Haven, Conn • Waterville, Maine • London

GALE
CENGAGE Learning™

Christine Nasso, *Publisher*
Elizabeth Des Chenes, *Managing Editor*

© 2008 Greenhaven Press, a part of Gale, Cengage Learning.

For more information, contact:
Greenhaven Press
27500 Drake Rd.
Farmington Hills, MI 48331-3535
Or you can visit our Internet site at gale.cengage.com

LIBRARY OF CONGRESS CATALOGING-IN-PUBLICATION DATA

Military draft / Viqi Wagner, book editor.
     p. cm. -- Opposing Viewpoints
     Includes bibliographical references and index.
     ISBN-13: 978-0-7377-3824-7 (hardcover)
     ISBN-10: 0-7377-3824-3 (hardcover)
     ISBN-13: 978-0-7377-3825-4 (pbk.)
     ISBN-10: 0-7377-3825-1 (pbk.)
     1. Draft--United States. 2. Military service, Voluntary--United States. I. Wagner, Viqi, 1953-
     UB323.M5367 2008
     355.2'23630973--dc22
                                                                    2007038960

Printed in the United States of America
3 4 5 6 7 12 11 10 09

Contents

Why Consider Opposing Viewpoints?   11

Introduction   14

Chapter 1: Should the United States Reinstate the Draft?

Chapter Preface   19

1. The United States Should Reinstate the Draft   21
   Walter L. Stewart Jr.

2. Reinstating the Draft Is Not Necessary   32
   Bernard D. Rostker

3. All-Volunteer Recruitment Is Not   42
   Supplying Enough Troops
   Phillip Carter and Paul Glastris

4. All-Volunteer Recruitment Can   53
   Supply Enough Troops
   Lawrence J. Korb

5. A Draft Is Cheaper Than Financing   63
   the All-Volunteer Military
   Julian E. Barnes and Peter Spiegel

6. A Draft Is More Costly Than Financing   70
   the All-Volunteer Military
   John C. Goodman

7. The Army's Stop-Loss Policy Is   79
   a "Back-Door" Draft
   Christopher Hayes

8. The Army's Stop-Loss Policy Is a Legal   86
   Extension of Voluntary Enlistment
   Daniel C. Brown

Periodical Bibliography   94

Chapter 2: How Would the Draft Affect U.S. Society?

Chapter Preface   96

1. A Draft Would Unify U.S. Society   98
   Hodding Carter and Ronald Goldfarb

2. A Draft Would Divide U.S. Society   102
   David Greenberg

3. A Draft Would Improve Declining   109
   Troop Quality
   Michelle Cottle

4. There Is No Evidence That Troop Quality   115
   Has Declined in the All-Volunteer Army
   Tim Kane

Periodical Bibliography   123

Chapter 3: Who Should Be Subject to a Military Draft?

Chapter Preface   125

1. Women Should Be Eligible for the Draft   127
   Philip Gold and Erin Solaro

2. Women Should Not Be Eligible for the Draft   134
   R. Cort Kirkwood

3. The Military Should Accept   143
   Open Homosexuals
   John M. Shalikashvili

4. The Military Should Not Accept   148
   Open Homosexuals
   J. Matt Barber

5. Draftees Should Be Selected by Lottery   153
   Alliance for Security

6. Draftees Could Be Selected for Critical,   **160**
   Specialized Skills
   Charles S. Abell et al.

Periodical Bibliography   **165**

Chapter 4: Should Alternatives to the Military Draft Be Pursued?

Chapter Preface   **167**

1. Universal National Service Should Replace   **170**
   the Selective Service System
   William A. Galston

2. Universal National Service Is a Bad Idea   **184**
   Bruce Chapman

3. Revive the ROTC Program to Expand   **195**
   the All-Volunteer Armed Forces
   Stanley Kurtz

4. Recruitment of Foreigners Would   **200**
   Boost Military Ranks
   Bryan Bender

5. The U.S. Military Can Hire Private Contractors   **207**
   Michelle Gutiérrez

6. The United States Should Not Pursue   **212**
   Military Expansion
   Gordon Adams

Periodical Bibliography   **219**

For Further Discussion   **220**

Organizations to Contact   **223**

Bibliography of Books   **228**

Index   **232**

Why Consider Opposing Viewpoints?

"The only way in which a human being can make some approach to knowing the whole of a subject is by hearing what can be said about it by persons of every variety of opinion and studying all modes in which it can be looked at by every character of mind. No wise man ever acquired his wisdom in any mode but this."

John Stuart Mill

In our media-intensive culture it is not difficult to find differing opinions. Thousands of newspapers and magazines and dozens of radio and television talk shows resound with differing points of view. The difficulty lies in deciding which opinion to agree with and which "experts" seem the most credible. The more inundated we become with differing opinions and claims, the more essential it is to hone critical reading and thinking skills to evaluate these ideas. Opposing Viewpoints books address this problem directly by presenting stimulating debates that can be used to enhance and teach these skills. The varied opinions contained in each book examine many different aspects of a single issue. While examining these conveniently edited opposing views, readers can develop critical thinking skills such as the ability to compare and contrast authors' credibility, facts, argumentation styles, use of persuasive techniques, and other stylistic tools. In short, the Opposing Viewpoints series is an ideal way to attain the higher-level thinking and reading skills so essential in a culture of diverse and contradictory opinions.

In addition to providing a tool for critical thinking, Opposing Viewpoints books challenge readers to question their own strongly held opinions and assumptions. Most people form their opinions on the basis of upbringing, peer pressure, and personal, cultural, or professional bias. By reading carefully balanced opposing views, readers must directly confront new ideas as well as the opinions of those with whom they disagree. This is not to simplistically argue that everyone who reads opposing views will—or should—change his or her opinion. Instead, the series enhances readers' understanding of their own views by encouraging confrontation with opposing ideas. Careful examination of others' views can lead to the readers' understanding of the logical inconsistencies in their own opinions, perspective on why they hold an opinion, and the consideration of the possibility that their opinion requires further evaluation.

Evaluating Other Opinions

To ensure that this type of examination occurs, Opposing Viewpoints books present all types of opinions. Prominent spokespeople on different sides of each issue as well as well-known professionals from many disciplines challenge the reader. An additional goal of the series is to provide a forum for other, less known, or even unpopular viewpoints. The opinion of an ordinary person who has had to make the decision to cut off life support from a terminally ill relative, for example, may be just as valuable and provide just as much insight as a medical ethicist's professional opinion. The editors have two additional purposes in including these less known views. One, the editors encourage readers to respect others' opinions—even when not enhanced by professional credibility. It is only by reading or listening to and objectively evaluating others' ideas that one can determine whether they are worthy of consideration. Two, the inclusion of such viewpoints encourages the important critical thinking skill of objectively evaluating an author's credentials and bias. This evaluation will illuminate an author's reasons for taking a particular stance on an issue and will aid in readers' evaluation of the author's ideas.

It is our hope that these books will give readers a deeper understanding of the issues debated and an appreciation of the complexity of even seemingly simple issues when good and honest people disagree. This awareness is particularly important in a democratic society such as ours in which people enter into public debate to determine the common good. Those with whom one disagrees should not be regarded as enemies but rather as people whose views deserve careful examination and may shed light on one's own.

Thomas Jefferson once said that "difference of opinion leads to inquiry, and inquiry to truth." Jefferson, a broadly educated man, argued that "if a nation expects to be ignorant and free . . . it expects what never was and never will be." As individuals and as a nation, it is imperative that we consider the opinions of others and examine them with skill and discernment. The Opposing Viewpoints series is intended to help readers achieve this goal.

David L. Bender and Bruno Leone,
Founders

Introduction

> *"Conscription involves the degradation of human personality, and the destruction of liberty. . . . The State which thinks itself entitled to force its citizens to go to war will never pay proper regard to the value and happiness of their lives in peace."*
>
> —Anti-Conscription
> Manifesto of 1926, signed among others
> by Albert Einstein and M.K. Gandhi

> *"The principle of the draft which simply is involuntary, or enforced service, is not new. It has been practiced in all ages of the world. It was well known to the framers of our constitution as one of the modes of raising armies, at the time they placed in that instrument the provision that 'the congress shall have the power to raise and support armies.' It has been used, just before, in establishing our independence; and it was used under the constitution of 1812. Wherein is the peculiar hardship now?"*
>
> —Abraham Lincoln,
> 1863

The United States has raised armies through conscription, or mandatory military service, six times in its history, five in wartime and once during peacetime. The five wartime drafts have little in common: They occurred in two centuries. American draftees fought in different parts of the world, in different kinds of conflict, against different foreign enemies and once against each other. Some wars ended in victory, some in defeat, one in a stalemate. Yet there is at least one common factor in all draft eras: Conscription has always been a bitterly divisive issue and has always inspired a more or less vigorous antidraft movement.

Technically, conscription was used in the American Revolution, but only on a state-by-state basis when volunteers or paid substitutes did not fill the ranks of militias or Continental Army units. Not until the Civil War did the federal government exercise the authority to employ national conscription. Both sides intended to fight with volunteer armies but both sides turned to conscription when a quick victory did not materialize. The Confederate States instituted the draft first, in 1862; Southerners responded with widespread violent resistance and most draftees who could do so paid substitutes to take their place. In 1863 the Union instituted its first draft, sparking the most violent antidraft protests in U.S. history, mostly in New York City, where riots and arson killed at least a hundred people before federal troops put down the uprising. Union draft resisters mainly objected to the provision exempting a man from the draft if he paid a $300 commutation fee or supplied a substitute—then, as in later conflicts, draftees called the conflict "the rich man's war and the poor man's fight."

The Selective Service Act of 1917 required all men ages 21 to 45 to register for the draft, anticipating America's late entry into World War I, but for the first time allowed opponents of the draft to apply for conscientious objector (CO) status. Ultimately 4 million Americans were drafted into the army, but the war soon ended and most antiwar, antidraft sentiment was expressed in the early 1920s through the formation of organizations such as the War Resisters League.

It is a common misperception that in "good wars" such as World War II, conscription was universally uncontroversial and all draftees willingly reported for duty. It is true, as retired brigadier general John S. Brown reports:

> During World War II voluntary enlistment was suspended, virtually eliminating war-time distinctions between draftees and volunteers—and the prospect that volunteers would engineer better deals for themselves or benefit from a two-tiered system. . . . The most significant factors in the fairness of the World War II draft were the draft's pervasiveness and perceived inevitability. The United States ultimately put 16 million people in uniform out of a population of more than 130 million.

However, ardent pacifists did protest the war, especially in its early years before appeasement and isolationism failed and before the brutality of the Nazi regime was widely known.

Draft registration continued during the Cold War and the Selective Service Act was expanded in 1950 to permit conscription for the Korean War. Roughly 1.5 million men were drafted between 1950 and 1953, when a ceasefire was negotiated, antidraft sentiment was most clearly reflected in the fact that the number of men who applied for CO status during the Korean War—1.5 percent of all draftees—increased tenfold over the two world war eras.

Opposition to the draft peaked during the Vietnam War era, 1964–1973, and took a number of new forms. Once again, protesters objected that the draft was discriminatory; full of loopholes that exempted the wealthy, the well-connected, and the better educated; and disproportionately put the burden of fighting on the working class and the poor. Once again, many draftees applied for conscientious objector status. As the Vietnam War became increasingly controversial and unpopular, and graphic images from the conflict were first broadcast into Americans' living rooms, opposition to the draft became the focal point of the antiwar movement in general. Some 50,000 draft dodgers moved to Canada. Many antiwar demonstrations featured public draft-card burnings, and many draftees fought their induction in court. The intensity of the home-front antiwar, antidraft movement, which only increased after the Selective Service Agency introduced a lottery system in 1969, is cited as a major factor in both the withdrawal of the United States from Southeast Asia and the bitterness of returning veterans.

With the end of the Vietnam War came the end of the draft in 1973 and the transformation of the U.S. military to an all-volunteer force. Draft registration was reinstated in 1980, and rumors of the imminent reinstatement of the draft have circulated periodically, but today's young people have grown up in a nation without the draft. The antidraft movement subsided, until the terrorist attacks of 9/11 and subsequent U.S. military involvement in Afghanistan and Iraq again raised the issue of the fairest way to ensure the U.S. military has the manpower it needs in the war against terrorism.

The contributors to *Opposing Viewpoints: Military Draft* debate the political, ethical, and social justification for reviving conscription. They discuss issues in the following chapters: Should the United States Reinstate the Draft? How Would the Draft Affect U.S. Society? Who Should Be Subject to a Military Draft? and Should Alternatives to the Military Draft Be Pursued? In 2007 the tightly stretched all-volunteer force is fighting a protracted war in Iraq, deployed in more than 120 countries around the world, and expected to effectively respond to new foreign military conflicts as well as defend America's borders from foreign enemies. No force can indefinitely stretch without snapping; this book asks whether a military draft would relieve or exacerbate the tension.

OPPOSING
VIEWPOINTS®
SERIES

CHAPTER 1

Should the United States Reinstate the Draft?

Chapter Preface

The U.S. Army as of 2007 is stretched thin, some say to the breaking point. Approximately 350,000 troops, more than 60 percent of the army, are deployed in more than 120 countries: 64,000 in Germany; 33,400 in Japan; 49,000 in Kuwait; more than 31,000 in South Korea; 12,350 in Afghanistan and Pakistan; more than 10,000 each in Italy and the United Kingdom; roughly 1,550 each in Cuba, Bosnia, and Kosovo. As of May 2007, roughly 160,000 army personnel are stationed in Iraq, where the conflict once projected to last for a few months continues into its fourth year.

The main consequences of the strain are that soldiers are going into combat zones with less training, and units are being redeployed with much less time between tours of duty. As *Time* reporter Mark Thompson wrote in April 2007, in the rush to get the four-thousand-troop 1st Brigade to the war zone, the standard four-week pre-Iraq combat training that was supposed to follow nine weeks of basic training was replaced by a ten-day course on "weapon use, first aid, and Iraqi culture. That's the same length as the course that teaches soldiers assigned to generals' household staffs the finer points of table service." Instead of a two-year break between combat tours, some army units are returning to Iraq after eleven months at home, a turnaround that critics charge is contributing to a 50 percent increase in combat stress over soldiers in units that have deployed once and notable increases in desertions and army suicides. Analysts such as retired general Walter L. Stewart Jr. have called for reinstating the military draft to relieve the strain on active-duty personnel and a realistic reassessment of a war that has proved neither quick nor easy.

But critical shortfalls are occurring in gear and weapons as well as troops; equipment is both in short supply at home and in deteriorating condition in the field. Thomson reports, for example, that equipment stockpiles are shrinking as their contents are shipped to Iraq, and insurgents' improvised explosive devices (IEDs) are improved just as quickly as their Humvee targets' armor is strengthened. A January 2007 report says troops have "experienced shortages of force-protection equipment . . . electronic countermeasure devices . . . weapons and communications equipment." Weapons and equipment shortages prompt critics such as Lawrence Korb to charge that a military draft will not relieve the thinly stretched army if it cannot adequately train and protect the soldiers it already has.

Defense experts have suggested several solutions to the army's personnel problems, including defense budget hikes, retooling tactics in favor of lengthy guerrilla campaigns and away from all-out tank battles along well-defined front lines, and withdrawal from Iraq to rebuild the tired volunteer force. The contributors to the following chapter consider whether a military draft is the answer.

> *"Now is the time to fix a horrendous national mistake by returning to the just and awesome deterrent power of a draft-induced military."*

The United States Should Reinstate the Draft

Walter L. Stewart Jr.

In the following viewpoint, retired major general Walter L. Stewart Jr. calls the all-volunteer military a failed experiment that threatens the viability of the nation. The claim that today's armed forces are more effective because volunteers "want to be there" is a fallacy, Stewart maintains: Even after lowering personnel standards and paying enlistees more money, the army can't recruit enough people to maintain an active force of 500,000, and the carnage inflicted in Iraq by rudimentary, outdated weapons shows how dangerous it is to believe sophisticated technology and a "leaner" military can take the place of more boots on the ground. Too few junior officers and enlistees are being asked to do too much hard duty, at great operational and moral cost, he warns, and the lessons of history show that enemies will not hesitate to attack when they see how stretched, and how weak, U.S. defenses are becoming. He urges a politically

Walter L. Stewart Jr., "The All Volunteer Army: Can We Still Claim Success?" *Military Review*, July-August 2006, pp. 101–107. Copyright © 2006 U.S. Army CGSC. Reproduced by permission.

palatable return to the draft in the form of regulated state militias and reorganized reserve components. Walter L. Stewart Jr. commanded the 28th Infantry Division of the Army National Guard among other command and staff positions in the United States and Europe.

As you read, consider the following questions:

1. What false premise led to the abandonment of the draft in 1973, according to Stewart?
2. How does the author use the examples of World War II and the Korean War to dispute Secretary of Defense Caspar Weinberger's claim that "volunteers were far more effective than draftees"?
3. Why does Stewart call draft-critics' claim that the United States has only conscripted its armed forces for a few years of its history a false notion?

In 1974, after just 20 months of experience, the all-volunteer Army was declared a success. But this was based solely on recruitment after a sustained period of combat had ended and at the beginning of an extended period of relatively secure garrison and peacekeeping duty, interspersed by short-duration conflicts.

But can we continue to claim success in 2006 when we consider a U.S. population increase of roughly 100 million since 1974, the near doubling of the recruiting pool because of the opening of most military occupations to females, and deployments that, although dangerous, are not nearly as perilous as previous prolonged conflicts? I say we cannot, and I offer as proof the continuing modifications. of personnel standards and the expansion of monetary inducements to achieve the Pyrrhic victory of recruiting 80,000 to an Active Component strength that resists expansion beyond 500,000, with junior officers and enlisted personnel stoically facing one hardship tour followed closely by another.

After 3 decades, our national experiment with an all-volunteer force has foundered during its first encounter with combat operations that last for an extended period of time. And accompanying this turn of events come consequences of even greater proportion: dangers to the viability of our nation itself now that it raises its army in contravention of the lessons of its history and that of Western civilization.

In the opening pages of *The Decline and Fall of the Roman Empire*, historian Edward Gibbon describes the essential nature of government: "Civil governments, in their first institutions, are voluntary associations for mutual defense. To obtain the desired end, it is absolutely necessary that each individual regard himself obligated to submit his private opinion and actions to the judgment of the greater number of his associates."

Gibbon knew that armies define nations and that volunteerism in an armed service should extend only to the voluntary submission of individual will to the collective will. This is a paradox to be examined. At a time in history when technology-intensive interstate conflict seems in decline, conflict requiring the low-tech actions of the squad and platoon is in ascension. In a tragedy of bad timing, in the 3 decades following the Vietnam War, recruitment of American forces discounted the human and cultural sciences in favor of the impersonal (but predictable) "supply and demand" science of markets: "Need more, pay more. Cannot pay more?—Make do with less, or substitute."

Symbolic confirmation of this "boots on the ground" predicament is everywhere. Men and women in uniform are treated universally as scarce and even iconic commodities; the political or strategic level of war is compressed, deferentially, into the operational and tactical with the ethical and moral consequences of sending American youth into harm's way subtly dismissed by statements such as "They are volunteers and want to be there." Operational commanders who know the scarcity and fragility of squads, platoons, and companies are unjustly required to make war decisions at the theater-force and ultimate victory levels. How did we arrive at such a state?

Act in Haste

In 1970, economists Alan Greenspan and Milton Friedman joined with other presidential appointees to officially deny the likelihood of negative consequences arising from the national move to an all-volunteer force. But these negative consequences are now evident and felt most heavily at the operational and tactical levels of war.

The great national experiment with an all-volunteer military is a failure that awaits truth or tragedy for confirmation. It relies on fewer and fewer to bear the blood burdens of defense, absolves the many of any fiscal, physical, or mental hardships, and, in a dawning age of asymmetric, non-state, and ascendant-state warfare, denies human power in favor of a near mystical belief in technology. We marvel at the sight and promise of an F-22 Raptor—even as we count the carnage caused by decades-old 155-millimeter rounds wired with field-expedient detonators and detonated by barely trained cultural warriors. Cultural war (for example, Western liberalism versus Soviet tyranny) requires the mobilization and commitment of cultures. Although we know how to do this, we lack even the courage for bloodless debate. . . .

History records that the decision to move to an all-volunteer force, then form a commission charged with justifying it, was based on a false premise, the myth of class-based "draft inequity," which was formally presented to [President Richard M.] Nixon in January 1969, during a meeting in the Oval Office with Reverend Theodore M. Hesburgh, president, University of Notre Dame, and member of the U.S. Commission on Civil Rights. Hesburgh describes the moment and the strategic wheels it placed in motion: "The thing I advised [Nixon] was to end the war in Vietnam soon. He said he was going to do that. Then I recommended giving the vote to eighteen-year-olds. Third, I said he should abolish the draft, because it was inequitable. Poor blacks and Hispanics were being drafted into the Army while most whites typically had all kinds of ways to beat it. I said we should be moving toward an all-volunteer Army . . . two weeks after that, I got [a] call . . . from Tom Gates, the former Secretary of the Navy and a very dear friend of mine. He did not ask, he ordered me to join his newly created Commission on an All-Volunteer Armed Force. 'This was your bright idea,' Gates said. 'You talked Nixon into it, and now I'm the chairman. So because you opened your mouth, I'm putting you on the commission.'"

There you have it: This was the moment of conception of the "they want to be there" military. The unscientific and badly off-the-mark conclusions of a sincere man of God were instrumental in detaching American citizens from the hardships or consequences of military service. The great, republican equity of our draft and draft-induced armies was abandoned because of a false perception of racial and social inequity. By decisions such as these, cultures and the armies that sustain them are lost.

Commission Dismissals

To support his policy decision, Nixon's commissioners studied, discussed, pondered, and promptly dismissed every one of the following legitimate objections to an all-volunteer Army:

- An all-volunteer force will be very costly—so costly the Nation cannot afford it.

- The all-volunteer force will lack the flexibility to expand rapidly in times of crisis.

- An all-volunteer force will undermine patriotism by weakening the traditional belief that each citizen has a moral responsibility to serve his country.

25

- The presence of draftees in a mixed force guard against the growth of a separate military ethos, which could pose a threat to civilian authority, our freedom, and our democratic institutions.

- The higher pay required for a voluntary force will be especially appealing to blacks who have relatively poorer civilian opportunities. This, combined with higher reenlistment rates for blacks, will mean that a disproportionate number of them will be in military service. White enlistments and reenlistments might decline, leading to an all-black enlisted force. U.S. racial tensions would grow because of white apprehension at this development and black resentment at bearing an undue share of the burden of defense. At the same time, some of the most qualified blacks would be in the military—not in the community where their talents are needed.

- Those joining an all-volunteer force will be men from the lowest economic classes, motivated primarily by monetary rewards rather than patriotism. An all-volunteer force will be manned, in effect, by mercenaries.

- An all-volunteer force would stimulate foreign military adventures, foster an irresponsible foreign policy, and lessen civilian concern about the use of military forces.

- A voluntary force will be less effective because not enough highly qualified youths will enlist and pursue military careers. As the quality of servicemen declines, the prestige and dignity of the services will also decline and further intensify recruiting problems.

A Three-Tiered Draft for the 21st Century

A draft for the 21st century is the only answer to our national security needs. Such a draft would have three tiers of youth service, with 18-month tours of duty for citizens ages 18 to 25. The first tier would be modeled after a standard military draft. The second tier would be for homeland security, such as guarding our borders, ports, nuclear installations and chemical plants. Included in this category would be police officers, firefighters, air marshals and disaster medical technicians. The third tier would be for civilian national service, such as the Peace Corps, AmeriCorps, Habitat for Humanity, Teach for America, assistance for the elderly and infirm, environmental work and the like. Women should be draft-eligible for the latter two categories and, of course, can volunteer for military service as now.

Charles Moskos, "Feel That Draft?"
Chicago Tribune, *June 9, 2005.*

- The defense budget will not be increased to provide for an all-volunteer force, and the Department of Defense (DOD) will have to cut back expenditures in other areas. Even if additional funds are provided initially, competing demands will, over the long term, force DOD to absorb the added budgetary expense of an all-volunteer force. The result could be serious deterioration of the nation's overall military posture. . . .

Resetting the Force

In spite of the patriotism and sacrifice of our men and women in uniform, a national military policy built on a false supposition will—like a line of horse cavalry that has outlived its usefulness but not the heart's expectation—fail at the most critical of moments. The national decision to move to an all-volunteer force, built on the falsity of draft inequity, is this line of cavalry—a line barely able to sustain combat in Southwest Asia, let alone expand to the East.

To preclude cataclysmic failure, we must return to an army that sustained itself during 17 years of cold war combat in Korea and Vietnam, suffered over 94,000 killed in the process, deterred the Soviet Union to the point of collapse, and maintained its morale and courage at the tactical level of war until overwhelmed by policy failure at the strategic level. This army was a draft-induced army, and there is a politically palatable way to have it back, but we must first counter the falsities that caused its loss.

In a *Wall Street Journal* article on 10 January 2003, former Secretary of Defense Caspar W. Weinberger—calling on his enlisted and junior officer experience in World War II to advise against a return to a draft—makes a blatantly ill-informed observation: "There was no doubt in anyone's mind that volunteers were far more effective than draftees and eager to train and fight." If we are to take Weinberger's observation at face value, one wonders how the United States prevailed over Nazi tyranny and Japanese imperialism, because in World War II, 93 percent of Army personnel were draftees. And considering young Weinberger held low-ranking soldier positions—positions and ranks nearest the draftee—one wonders where he observed the voluntary 7 percent of the Army that was "more effective . . . and eager to train and fight." The legitimacy of Weinberger's argument collapses under cursory review, but it joins with equally fallacious "draft inequity" arguments to underpin a policy blunder that has our nation reeling, and enemies more powerful than the 10,000 terrorists in Iraq biding their time and salivating.

The March 2003 *VFW Magazine* summarizes the service and sacrifice of the Vietnam-era draftee: During the Vietnam era, 1,728,344 men were drafted. Of the forces who actually served in Vietnam, 648,500 (25 percent) were draftees. Draftees (17,725) accounted for 30.4 percent of combat deaths in Vietnam.

Other than lending credence to former British Prime Minister James Callaghan's observation that "a lie can be half-way round the world before the truth has got its boots on," anti-draft arguments (such as that put forth by Weinberger) are without merit. But as myth, they did meld with "class war" falsities to demean the record of the Vietnam-era Army in its entirety, and the men and women who formed it, individually. These soldiers were the sons and daughters of the World War II generation, and to believe that the Army they formed was consumed by rampant drug use, open racial tension, and general indiscipline is to believe that this is how the "Greatest Generation" raised their children. Yes, leaders in the Vietnam-era Army had to deal with drugs and other soldier failings—just as leaders in our present Army must—but negative factors then were no more consumptive than they are now, and one can only speculate whether a volunteer army—abandoned during a decade-long war and after suffering more than 50,000 killed—would do any better. I say it would not—a conclusion I make by measuring the actions now being taken to sustain our Army during the Global War on Terrorism.

Now is the time to fix a horrendous national mistake by returning to the just and awesome deterrent power of a draft-induced military. (Time is short because only a dreamer could imagine an army sustaining itself in war against tens-of-thousands when it can barely sustain itself in war against a few thousand terrorists.) A politically palatable way exists to return to the draft. But first we must dispel another false notion—that, collectively and historically, the draft has only served this country for a few years. This notion ignores the compelled-service nature of colonial and state militias and decades of service under the command of colonial and state governors. During much of American history, compulsory militia service was a fact of life. It militarized U.S. culture in a way that was non-threatening to the Homeland, but quite threatening to potential enemies. The militia's existence and inducement effects were critical to rapidly forming regular forces during times of war. Army Rangers take their name from militia "ranging units" that countered French and Indian depredations. The English colonists and the rifle companies that joined New England militias at Boston in 1775 to form the United States Army found their recruiting base in the militia organizations of frontier America.

The Nation can follow this precedent. It can "draft" for the regulated militias of the states—the National Guards. A draft for Guard service will find political support, if done in conjunction with a reorganization of the Reserve Components. The Army Reserve should transfer its troop-unit programs to the Army National Guard; the Air National Guard to the Air Force Reserve; and the Chief of the National Guard Bureau must be elevated to four-star rank, made a member of the Joint Chiefs of Staff, and designated as commander of Northern Command.

The political will to see these things through will come from the governors of the states, 50 commanders in chief who will gain troop units that lend themselves to state contingencies (absent Posse Comitatus prohibitions, of course) in exchange for fighter, tanker, and air cargo units that do not. No general officer, adjutant general, soldier, or airman will lose his or her position. Reserve forces available for federal service will be unchanged: the inducement effect of the draft, as it always has, will sustain regular forces; and the patriotic appeal of drafting for homeland defense and contingencies will fill draft calls with willing youth.

These things are possible; events have proven that sustaining the all-volunteer force is not. And it is overstretched junior leaders who must find the will to vocal advocacy, because years ago, senior leaders were ordered "aboard" and know there is only one way off. [i.e., they will lose face and their positions if they break ranks and oppose the all-volunteer military]. If they find the will to do so, young officers will once again command Washington's "army of the constitution," and our Republic will avoid history's condemnation.

> The past 30 years ... have proven that
> an all-volunteer force can be sustained
> in peace and during the initial periods
> of military conflict.

Reinstating the Draft
Is Not Necessary

Bernard D. Rostker

*Bernard D. Rostker is a senior fellow at the RAND Corporation,
a nonpartisan public policy think tank in Santa Monica, California. He has held several senior government posts, including assistant secretary of the U.S. Navy, undersecretary of the U.S.
Army, and undersecretary of defense for personnel and readiness.
In the following viewpoint, Rostker argues that the all-volunteer
military has been an unqualified success: Compared to the U.S.
military in 1973, the year the draft was ended, the U.S. military
of the early 2000s has more education, higher intelligence-test
scores, more ethnic and gender balance, and higher socioeconomic status. Rostker credits good leadership, better analytical
tools to make sure new policies are necessary and effective before
making changes, high-quality inducements that boost reenlistment, and adequate budgets for this success. He disputes critics*

Bernard D. Rostker, "Steady Under Fire: All-Volunteer Force Proves Its Resilience, So
Far," *RAND Review*, Fall 2006. Copyright © 2006 RAND Corporation. Republished
with permission of *RAND Review*, conveyed through Copyright Clearance Center, Inc.

who say an armed force in a major conflict cannot be voluntary; he maintains with some qualification that despite falling recruitment levels and protracted conflicts in Iraq and Afghanistan, the all-volunteer military is doing the job, and reinstating the draft would be a costly, unnecessary, bad idea.

As you read, consider the following questions:

1. During how much of its history has the United States actually conscripted its armed forces, according to Rostker?

2. How does Rostker dispute the claim that volunteers will not reenlist knowing they will likely have to reenter a combat zone?

3. What's wrong with reinstating the draft in the form of universal national service, according to the author?

America's all-volunteer military has been an overwhelming success since its inception in 1973, but the force faces an unprecedented challenge posed by the wars in Iraq and Afghanistan. The all-volunteer military has become the world's strongest fighting force, attracting recruits who are better educated and more skilled than those who served under the U.S. military draft. However, after four years of war with mounting casualties in Iraq, continuing insurgent attacks in Iraq and Afghanistan, and multiple additional deployments throughout the world, the all-volunteer force has experienced recruiting shortfalls for the first time since the late 1970s.

To date, the all-volunteer force has done the job. Under the draft, people served because we in America made them serve. Under the all-volunteer force, people serve because they want to serve, and they are serving very well in the most trying of circumstances. Short of a total collapse of the system, there is no better way to, in the words of the U.S. Constitution, "raise and support armies" and "provide and maintain a navy."

The all-volunteer force has shown it can be successful during periods of conflict as well as during peacetime. Nevertheless, the sustained conflicts in the Middle East pose obstacles not faced before. Reenlistment rates have remained high in spite of the wars in Iraq and Afghanistan, sustaining the overall size of the force. But the U.S. Army, Army National Guard, and Army Reserve have faced difficulty recruiting new personnel. There are no guarantees with a volunteer force. Only time will tell if the current level of operations can be sustained into the future.

The volunteer force has proven much more resilient than we had any reason to hope it would be and has far exceeded the early estimates of those who put it into place. But logic tells us there is a limit. Just because we have not yet broken the force does not mean it cannot be broken.

Evolution of the All-Volunteer Force

The United States has conscripted its armed forces for only 35 of its 230 years—nearly all in the 20th century—and the American people have been generally willing to accept the practice of conscription when service has been perceived to be universal. That acceptance began to erode in the 1960s. There were five major reasons:

- *Demographics.* The size of the eligible population of young men reaching draft age each year was so large and the needs of the military so small in comparison that, in practice, the draft was no longer universal.

- *Cost.* Obtaining enough volunteers was possible at acceptable budget levels.

- *Moral and economic rationale.* Conservatives and libertarians argued that the state had no right to impose military service on young men without their consent. Liberals asserted that the draft placed unfair burdens on the underprivileged members of society, who were less likely to get deferments.

- *Opposition to the war in Vietnam.* The growing unpopularity of the Vietnam War meant the country was ripe for a change to a volunteer force.

- *The U.S. Army's desire for change.* The army had lost confidence in the draft as discipline problems among draftees mounted in Vietnam.

In 1969, President Richard Nixon created the President's Commission on an All-Volunteer Armed Force, also known as the Gates Commission. It considered key military-manpower issues, including personnel supply and demand, attrition and retention, and the ideal mix of career and noncareer members in the context of management efficiency and personal equity.

The commission concluded that the nation's interests would be better served by an all-volunteer force rather than by a combination of volunteers and conscripts. In 1971, Nixon signed a law to end the draft and to put the selective service structure on standby. After a two-year extension of induction authority, the end of the draft was formally announced in January 1973.

Changes for the Better

The quality of military personnel has improved since the end of the draft, as measured by scores on intelligence tests. The percentage of new recruits with high school diplomas has surged. The proportion of career personnel and the proficiency and professionalism of the force have also dramatically increased. A largely unexpected consequence of moving to a professional military with better pay was a higher rate of reenlistment and a sharp rise in the size of the career force relative to the overall force. At the same time, the all-volunteer force has made the military more representative of the nation as a whole.

For 26 years, the U.S. Department of Defense has reported annually on social representation in the U.S. military. The 2004 report noted the following:

- *Education level.* The most recent statistics show that 92 percent of new enlistees to the active-duty force are high school graduates. The figure for the reserve components is 87 percent. This compares favorably with both the 1973 goal of 45 percent and the 2002 civilian graduation rate of 79 percent. In addition, 95 percent of active-duty officers have baccalaureate degrees, and 38 percent have advanced degrees.

- *Mental aptitude.* Today's American military [as of 2004] scores well above the civilian population on standard tests of intelligence.

- *Marital status.* The larger career force means that the number of service members who are married has increased. Today, 49 percent of enlisted personnel are married, compared with 40 percent in 1973. Among active-duty officers, 68 percent are married.

- *Gender.* Today [2004], 15 percent of the active-duty enlisted force is female, compared with less than 2 percent when the draft ended. Sixteen percent of the officer corps is female. Despite these improvements, women are still underrepresented in the military.

- *Race and ethnicity.* In fiscal year 2002, African Americans were slightly overrepresented among new enlistees relative to the civilian population: 16

percent compared with 14 percent. However, this is considerably more equitable than was the 1973 level of 28 percent. Latinos are currently underrepresented, making up 16 percent of all civilians but only 11 percent of new enlistees.

- *Socioeconomic status.* Recruits come primarily from families in the middle or lower middle classes. Few recruits come from upper-income families, leading some to criticize the all-volunteer military. But historically, few people from elite backgrounds have ever served in the military except during times of mass mobilization such as occurred during World War II.

- *Geographic representation.* The South continues to be overrepresented, with more than 41 percent of enlistments compared with 35 percent of the civilian population.

Pillars of Success

America's experience with the all-volunteer force suggests four principal reasons for its success: leadership, analysis, targeted programs, and adequate budgets. Whenever one of these factors has been missing over the past 30 years, the force has faltered.

The first factor is leadership from top management. The all-volunteer force would not have come into being when it did without the leadership of President Nixon, who began the planning process and announced the formation of the Gates Commission within weeks of taking office in 1969.

Within the military, U.S. Army General Maxwell Thurman is considered by many as the single most important person in the history of the all-volunteer force, because he taught the Pentagon how to recruit. He often said that it may be called an all-volunteer force, but it is really an "all-recruited force."

A Draft Is Unnecessary

Conscription makes sense when huge numbers of recruits are needed, relative to the population. But in the last two decades, military recruits were, at most, only 15 percent of the 18-year-old population. Although the pace of military operations has increased, the manpower needed to conduct a given type of operation has declined owing to technological improvements. On top of this, the youth population is growing. Thus, there is no reason the military will need a large portion of American youth to serve in the foreseeable future.

Beth Asch, *"Should Uncle Sam Want You?"*
RAND Commentary, *February 9, 2003.*

More than any other uniformed leader, Thurman recognized throughout the 1980s that the military had to compete aggressively in the civilian labor market for American youth—and had to do so with the right tools based on market research and statistical analysis.

The second factor, then, is the use of quantitative analysis to test, adjust, and evaluate policies. Almost every change to the all-volunteer force has been made only after research demonstrated its likely effect. The research of the 1960s and early 1970s reassured decisionmakers that such a force might be possible at acceptable budget outlays. In the 1970s and 1980s, test programs demonstrated the value of advertising, educational incentives, and bonuses in encouraging enlistment. Analytical evidence later helped reform the compensation system.

Studies of enlistee test scores and job performance proved what now seems logical but was once very controversial: People who score higher on standardized tests do better on the job than do those who score lower. The resulting emphasis on quality attracted capable people and led to the increasing professionalism of the military. And ever since the fall of the Soviet Union in 1991, which eliminated the threat that had dominated national security strategy for four decades, personnel research has helped defense managers make the adjustments necessary to transform the post–Cold War force into a smaller, more agile, and more engaged one.

The third factor is the implementation of targeted programs to attract the required types and numbers of recruits. To appeal to high-quality youths, the services had to craft marketing strategies and advertising campaigns that conveyed the benefits of military service; offer money for education, bonuses for enlisting in certain occupations, and enlistment tours of different lengths; and provide career opportunities that had civilian relevance. The services also had to train a professional and motivated recruiting staff. Finally, the key to creating a truly outstanding force was persuading the most capable members to reenlist. Careerists demanded not just good pay but also quality-of-life benefits, such as good housing, child care, health benefits, family advocacy programs, and military stores. It was crucial that the services become "family friendly."

The fourth factor required for success is adequate financial resources. The defense budget must be large enough to accomplish three things at once: support pay raises that keep pace with both inflation and civilian-sector pay increases; provide resources for advertising, recruiters, bonuses, and educational benefits; and fund the military retirement program and quality-of-life initiatives.

Old Questions Resurface

In 1969, Crawford Greenewalt, a member of the Gates Commission, shared his misgivings in a memorandum to the chairman, former Secretary of Defense Thomas Gates Jr. "While there is a reasonable possibility that a peacetime armed force could be entirely voluntary," wrote Greenewalt, "I am certain that an armed force involved in a major conflict could *not* be voluntary." So far, Greenewalt's reservations have not been borne out.

But given [in late 2006] the ongoing war in Iraq—with casualties rising, enlistments dropping, deployments being extended, the situation on the ground deteriorating, and a majority of the American public no longer believing that the war is worth fighting—the issue of recruiting enough volunteers to maintain the U.S. military at required levels is again relevant. With nearly 150,000 U.S. troops in Iraq and Afghanistan today, military commanders point to the outstanding job being done in these nontraditional conflicts. Remarkably, while enlistments have fallen off, retention remains at historically high levels. There were initial fears that soldiers would not reenlist if they had to deploy twice into combat zones. Yet some soldiers are now completing their third and fourth tours. U.S. troops have demonstrated their continuing commitment and willingness to serve.

Some critics say that one solution to the current dilemma would be to reinstate the draft as part of a universal system requiring all young people to commit time to national service of some type. But creating a system to employ all four million young people who reach adulthood every year would be very costly, if such a system were to be universal. And if not everyone were to serve, we would be in the same quandary in which we found ourselves during the 1960s.

A final judgment on the all-volunteer force has not been made. The 40-year partnership between policymakers and policy analysts has produced not only the finest fighting force the United States has ever fielded but also one that is broadly representative of the American people. The past 30 years—particularly the experiences in Iraq and Afghanistan—have proven that an all-volunteer force can be sustained in peace and during the initial periods of military conflict. Whether or not an all-volunteer force can be sustained over longer periods of ongoing conflicts and recurring deployments, as in the current situation, has yet to be determined.

> "America's all-volunteer military simply cannot deploy and sustain enough troops to succeed in places like Iraq while still deterring threats elsewhere in the world."

All-Volunteer Recruitment Is Not Supplying Enough Troops

Phillip Carter and Paul Glastris

Even if the wars in Afghanistan and Iraq had not required an indefinitely sustained force of more than 150,000 U.S. troops, the U.S. military is seriously shorthanded and ill-equipped to mobilize for either regional conflicts or threats to its own borders, Phillip Carter and Paul Glastris argue in the following viewpoint. Potential crises in North Korea, Taiwan, the Sudan, or any number of unforeseen situations could quickly exhaust the army's ability to respond, they maintain: Stepped-up recruitment of volunteers cannot solve "the short-term problem (too few troops now) without creating long-term problems (too many troops later)" when a huge standing army is no longer needed. The authors conclude that the draft is the time-tested best way to provide the military with high-quality ground forces in war-

Phillip Carter and Paul Glastris, "The Case for the Draft," *Washington Monthly*, March 2005. Copyright 2005 by Washington Monthly Publishing, LLC, 733 15th St. NW, Suite 520, Washington DC 20005. (202) 393-5155. www.washingtonmonthly.com. Reproduced by permission.

time without a huge military budget in peacetime. Phillip Carter is an attorney and former army captain who writes on national security issues for the Washington Monthly. *Paul Glastris is the editor in chief of the* Washington Monthly.

As you read, consider the following questions:

1. Carter and Glastris acknowledge that the U.S. military comprises 1.4 million active-duty troops and 870,900 reservists; why then do they say we don't have enough troops to sustain a force of 150,000 in Iraq?
2. Why do the authors argue that the U.S. military must have three to four soldiers for every soldier serving in places where a sustained force is needed for longer than a year or two, such as Iraq?
3. What kind of war is the all-volunteer army designed to fight, according to Carter and Glastris?

America's all-volunteer military simply cannot deploy and sustain enough troops to succeed in places like Iraq while still deterring threats elsewhere in the world. Simply adding more soldiers to the active duty force, as some in Washington are now suggesting, may sound like a good solution. But it's not, for sound operational and pragmatic reasons. America doesn't need a bigger standing army; it needs a deep bench of trained soldiers held in reserve who can be mobilized to handle the unpredictable but inevitable wars and humanitarian interventions of the future. And while there are several ways the all-volunteer force can create some extra surge capacity, all of them are limited.

The only effective solution to the manpower crunch is the one America has turned to again and again in its history: the draft. Not the mass combat mobilizations of World War II, nor the inequitable conscription of Vietnam—for just as threats change and war-fighting advances, so too must the draft. A modernized draft would demand that the privileged participate. It would give all who serve a choice over how they serve. And it would provide the military, on a "just in time" basis, large numbers of deployable ground troops, particularly the peacekeepers we'll need to meet the security challenges of the 21st century.

America has a choice. It can be the world's superpower, or it can maintain the current all-volunteer military, but it probably can't do both.

Plowing a Field with a Ferrari

Before the invasion of Iraq, Army Chief of Staff Eric Shinseki and Army Secretary Thomas White advised [then-Secretary of Defense Donald] Rumsfeld that many more troops would be needed to secure Iraq (something on the order of 250,000 to 300,000). Secretary of State Colin Powell, whose State Department was shut out of the post-war planning process, also privately argued for a bigger force. A RAND Corporation analysis, published in summer 2003, offered a range of estimates for what size force would be necessary in Iraq. Using troops-to-population ratios from previous occupations, RAND projected that, two years after the invasion, it would take anywhere from 258,000 troops (the Bosnia model), to 321,000 (post-World War II Germany), to 526,000 (Kosovo) to secure the peace.

None of these figures seems, at first glance, unachievable for a U.S. military comprised of 1.4 million active-duty troops, 870,900 reservists, and 110,000 individual ready reservists (soldiers who have served their tour of duty and are not training with the reserves but who can by statute still be called up for service). And yet an Iraq deployment that has never exceeded 153,000 ground personnel has put so much stress on the military that a senior Army Reserve official has candidly stated that current rotation policies will lead to a "broken force." How can that be? To answer that question, begin by deducting virtually the entire Navy and Air Force from the head count; the Iraq occupation has been almost exclusively a ground game, hence an Army and Marine operation. Next, consider that the United States sends into combat not individual soldiers but units, complete with unit equipment sets, unit leaders, and an organizational structure that facilitates command, control, and logistical support. So instead of counting individual soldiers—a meaningless exercise—one must look at how many units the United States could theoretically put on the ground if it wanted to mobilize every active and reserve soldier available. And if you do that, you come to a figure of roughly 600,000 troops. That's the total number of deployable soldiers that the United States could theoretically have called upon to man the initial invasion.

In practice, however, the Pentagon would never have sent that many troops to Iraq, for good reasons: It would have left the defense cupboard bare and served as an open invitation to America's enemies to make trouble elsewhere in the world. Massing a 600,000 force would have meant not only pulling nearly all front-line troops out of Korea, but also mobilizing the poorly-resourced divisions of the National Guard, the third-string crew that the president can call on when the first string (active troops) and the second string (the Guard's elite "enhanced" reserve brigades) are depleted.

Given the need to hold troops in reserve for deterrence purposes, the Pentagon had perhaps 400,000 troops available for the invasion. Yet that number includes many troops in specialized fields that are of little or no use in desert warfare or peacekeeping—off-loading equipment in sea ports, for instance. Such troops could have been reshaped into provisional infantry units, as the Army has done with artillery and air-defense formations, but that would've taken time. The number of troops with units that would actually have been of use in Iraq was probably closer to the figures that Gen. Shinseki and Secretary White have suggested: 250,000 to 300,000—in other words, the lower end of what RAND estimated would be required for success.

Initial Deployment Is Different from Sustained Deployment

But even that number is deceptive. It is the size of the force that could have been initially sent into Iraq, not the number that could have realistically been sustained there. Because so many soldiers in the all-volunteer military are married with families (compared to conscript armies), and because soldiers must periodically be induced or persuaded to voluntarily re-enlist, the Pentagon must rotate its forces in and out of theater every 12 months or so in order to maintain morale and reenlistment. Thus, just as a civilian police department must hire three to four police officers for every one cop on the beat, so too must the U.S. military have three to four soldiers for every one serving in Iraq.

The Pentagon, then, could have realistically kept those initial 250,000 to 300,000 troops in place only for a limited time—perhaps a year, certainly not more than two. That might have been enough time to pacify the country, especially if higher troop numbers at the outset would have quelled the early looting and disorder. Then again, a year or two might not have been sufficient time to beat back an insurgency which, we now know, was to some extent planned in advance of the invasion. In that case, keeping 250,000 to 300,000 troops in Iraq for two years or longer would have risked so lowering morale and reenlistment rates as to destroy the all-volunteer force. It would have been like plowing a field with a Ferrari; it could have been done, but only once. Taking the need for rotations into account, then, the U.S. military can comfortably handle something like 80,000 troops in Iraq at any one time. The actual number on the ground averaged 133,286 [from 2003–2005], and more than 150,000 soldiers are in Iraq [in March 2005].

That's a woefully insufficient number for the task. Yet it is pushing the outside limits of what the current force structure can handle. It has meant imposing "stop-loss" emergency measures to prevent soldiers from exiting the service. It has required deploying nearly every active-duty brigade, including one previously committed elsewhere in Korea. It has meant raiding the seed corn of military readiness by deploying the Army's elite "opposing force" training units—seasoned soldiers who play the enemy in mock exercises to build the skills of greener troops before they are sent into battle. It has necessitated calling up all 15 of the National Guard's enhanced readiness brigades, as well as poorly-resourced National Guard divisions that have not been mobilized en masse since the Korean War. It has led the Army Reserve Chief Lt. Gen. James Helmly to write in a [2005] memo that the Reserve will be unable to meet its commitments without substantial use of the Army's involuntary mobilization authorities under federal law. As of Dec. 15, 2004, the Army Reserve retained just 37,515 deployable soldiers out of a total of 200,366—almost no cushion at all. And in the final two months of [2004], the Reserves missed their enlistment targets by 30 percent—a sign of even greater problems to come.

All this for a war that most planners consider to be a medium-sized conflict—nothing like what the United States faced in World War I, World War II, or the Cold War. And while threats of that magnitude aren't anywhere on the horizon, there are plenty of quite possible scenarios that could quickly overwhelm us—an implosion of the North Korean regime, a Chinese attack on Taiwan, worsening of the ethnic cleansing in the Sudan, or some unforeseen humanitarian nightmare. Already we have signaled to bad actors everywhere the limits of our power. Military threats might never have convinced the Iranians to give up their nuclear program. But it's more than a little troubling that ruling Iranian mullahs

Critical Shortages of Equipment As Well As Personnel

The Iraq war ... has put unprecedented wear and tear on the Marine Corps' trucks, tanks and other combat equipment, according to a report by the Center for American Progress and the Lexington Institute, two policy research groups that frequently study national security issues. The war has forced the Marines to keep about 40 percent of its ground combat equipment, 50 percent of its communications gear and 20 percent of its aircraft in Iraq, the report says.

Helicopters fly two to three times more hours than they should, tanks are being used four times as much as anticipated, and Humvees are being driven an average of 480 miles a month, 70 percent of which is off-road. The harsh desert and combat losses are chewing up other gear at nine times their planned rates. Humvees that were expected to last 14 years need to be replaced after only four years in the extreme conditions of the Iraqi desert.

Tom Regan, "Backdoor Draft? 'Critical' Shortage Prompts
Involuntary Recall of Reservists by U.S. Marines,"
ChristianScienceMonitor.com, *August 23, 2006.*

can publicly and credibly dismiss recent administration saber-rattling by pointing to the fact that our forces are pinned down in Iraq.

Stress Test

Every 20 years or so for the past century, America has found it necessary, for national security reasons, to send at least half a million troops overseas into harm's way, and to keep them there for years at a time. It did so in World War I, sending 4.1 million doughboys and Marines to Europe. In World War II, it mobilized 16 million for the war effort. America sent more than 3 million grunts to fight in Korea against the North Koreans and Chinese, in the first hot war of the Cold War. It rotated 5.1 million soldiers and Marines through Vietnam over a decade, with 543,400 stationed there at the height of that war in April 1969. And more recently, America sent 550,000 ground troops to eject Saddam's forces from Kuwait, as part of a ground force which totaled 831,500 with allied contributions from dozens of nations. Along the way, the United States military simultaneously fought small wars in Greece, Lebanon, El Salvador, Somalia, Haiti, Bosnia, and Kosovo, requiring the commitment of thousands more. This ability to deploy large numbers of troops overseas for long periods of time has been the price of America's superpower status—what President John Kennedy alluded to in his inaugural address when he said America would bear any burden to assure the survival and the success of liberty. . . .

What we're increasingly learning from Iraq is that the all-volunteer force, as presently built, cannot do that—indeed, it was consciously designed to be incapable of such deployments. Today's force was built for precisely the kinds of wars that Caspar Weinberger and Colin Powell envisioned in their doctrines: wars with explicit purposes, narrow parameters, and clear exit strategies. In other words, it was built for the kinds of wars the military prefers to fight, not necessarily the kinds of wars we have, as a nation, historically fought. . . .

[After Vietnam], Pentagon leaders replaced the conscripted military with an all-volunteer force that would recruit enlistees with pay and benefits like the civilian world. This all-volunteer model, they believed, would improve morale for the simple reason that all soldiers would be in the service by choice. It would also improve military, effectiveness because if soldiers could be lured to stay longer by reenlisting, they could acquire higher levels of skill. The mantra of the new military became "send a bullet, not a man"; the modern

American military came to embrace precision firepower over manpower in what historian Russell Weigley called the "American way of war."

This all-volunteer military made good on nearly all these promises. After a rough period in the late 1970s, the U.S. military emerged a leaner, better force in the 1980s, proving itself in the small wars of that decade—Grenada, Libya, and Panama. Then came the first Gulf War—the apotheosis of the all-volunteer, total force model. Coming off the Cold War, the Army had 18 divisions on active duty, in comparison to 10 today, and had little in the way of a pressing commission with the imminent collapse of the Soviet Union. By mobilizing seven of these Army divisions and two Marine divisions, in addition to the reserves and ready reserves, military leaders were able to send half a million troops to the Saudi desert. But because that war lasted just months, largely due to U.S. reluctance to invade and occupy Iraq, the system worked. Active-duty soldiers deployed for less than a year, without fear of immediately being sent back to fight; reservists were similarly tapped just once. Desert Storm did not break the all-volunteer force because that war was precisely the kind that the force had been designed to fight: a limited campaign for limited ends, of limited duration, and with a defined exit strategy.

Unfortunately, national security threats don't always conform to the military's precise specifications. The 1990s brought two wars, in Bosnia and Kosovo, requiring the long-term commitment of U.S. troops for peacekeeping. These were relatively modest-sized deployments. Yet the military leadership complained that they put undo stress on the system, and, indeed, then-Gov. George Bush lambasted the Clinton administration in 2000 for the way it managed military readiness, charging that the Kosovo war put two of the Army's 10 divisions out of action, hurting the nation's ability to respond to threats abroad. In the wake of September 11, the U.S. military mobilized tens of thousands of reservists for homeland security and sent thousands of elite infantrymen and special forces into the mountains of Afghanistan; neither mission conformed to the model of past wars.

Then came Operation Iraqi Freedom, and the real stress test began. . . .

Only the Draft Fixes the Short- and Long-Term Problem

The United States does not necessarily need a massive standing military all the time. What it needs is a highly trained professional force of a certain size—what we have right now is fine—backed by a massive surge capacity of troops in reserve to quickly augment the active-duty force in times of emergency. Sure, right now, the Army is light several hundred thousand deployable ground troops. But over the long term, the demands of Iraq will subside, the need for troops will decline, and it could be another decade or two before another mission that big comes along.

The problem is that under the all-volunteer system it's hard to fix the short-term problem (too few troops now) without creating long-term problems (too many troops later). And so, paying for the salaries and benefits and families of 50,000 or 500,000 extra soldiers on active duty over the course of their careers doesn't, from a military standpoint, make sense. Politically, it would put the senior military leadership in the position of convincing the American people to keep military budgets extremely high to pay for a huge standing army that isn't being used and might not be for years. It might be possible now to convince the public to add another 100,000 soldiers (annual cost: about $10 billion in personnel costs alone, not including equipment and training). But the generals rightly worry that this support will evaporate after Iraq stabilizes. Indeed, Americans have a long tradition dating back to the writing of Constitution, of refusing to support a large standing military unless the need is apparent. (The public paid for a much bigger all-volunteer military in the 1970s and 1980s, but only because of the obvious need to deter a massive Soviet army from threatening Europe; after the Berlin Wall fell, both political parties supported big cuts in troop strength). What we really need is the capability to rapidly mobilize and deploy a half million troops to project U.S. power abroad, and to be able to sustain them indefinitely while maintaining a reserve with which to simultaneously engage other enemies. . . .

[The best option] for providing the military with sufficient numbers of high-quality deployable ground forces: conscription. America has nearly always chosen this option to staff its military in times of war. Today [2005], no leading politician in either party will come anywhere near the idea—the draft having replaced Social Security as the third rail of American politics. This will have to change if the United States is to remain the world's preeminent power.

> "Increasing the size of the Army and Marines will not help the situation on the ground in Iraq. Instead, growing these forces is about preparing America's forces for the future."

All-Volunteer Recruitment Can Supply Enough Troops

Lawrence J. Korb

Lawrence J. Korb is a senior fellow at the Center for American Progress and senior adviser to the Center for Defense Information in Washington, D.C. In the following April 2007 testimony before the Senate Armed Services Committee, Korb argues that the all-volunteer army is a highly trained and well-equipped initial response force that has been drained and misused in the ill-advised, protracted war in Iraq. Putting more troops in Iraq by reinstating the draft is not the answer, Korb says, when the army is not adequately training or protecting the troops it already has. Strengthening and expanding the military should continue on a volunteer basis, by restoring high recruitment standards, retention and promotion criteria, and ground force budgets; by opening up the services and all military occupations to all qualified people who want to serve, including women and homosexuals;

Lawrence J. Korb, "Testimony of Lawrence J. Korb," before the Senate Armed Services Committee, April 17, 2007. Reproduced by permission of the author.

and above all, by withdrawing from Iraq and focusing on building specialized peacekeeping and counterinsurgency brigades for the conflicts of the future.

As you read, consider the following questions:

1. How has the army violated its own deployment policy to sustain troop levels in Iraq, according to Korb?

2. What examples does Korb give to support his claim that soldiers are being rushed into the combat zone without adequate training and protection?

3. What barriers to volunteer service does the author say should be removed?

The current use of the ground forces in Iraq represents a complete misuse of the all-volunteer military. America's all-volunteer Army, made up of well-equipped and highly trained active-duty soldiers, backed up by a ready reserve, was designed to act as an initial response force, a force that would be able to repel and counter aggression. If America ever found itself in a long protracted ground war, or was forced to act against an existential threat, the all-volunteer force was to act as a bridge to re-instating conscription. This is why we require young men to register when they turn 18.

The all-volunteer force, particularly the Army component, as General John Abizaid noted last fall, was not "built to sustain a long war." Therefore, if the United States is going to have a significant component of its ground forces in Iraq over the next 5, 10, 15, or 30 years, then the responsible course is for the president and those supporting this open-ended and escalated presence in Iraq to call for re-instating the draft. That would be the responsible path.

In my view, however, this would be a mistake on par with the initial invasion of Iraq. Instead, I believe the United States should set a firm timetable for the gradual redeployment of

U.S. forces over the next 18 months. During that time the United States should work to train and support Iraqi security forces and the Iraqi government while gradually handing over responsibility for security to the Iraqis. This action should be backed up with a diplomatic surge in which the United States would engage all countries in the region. There is no guarantee that this approach will be effective in stabilizing Iraq or the region. In fact, given the misleading justifications for the initial invasion and the way in which the Bush administration has conducted the war, there are no good options left. But I believe that this course, a strategic redeployment and a diplomatic surge, provides the best chance for stabilizing the region as well as mitigating the impact of Iraq on the ground forces and U.S. national security. As General Maxwell Taylor noted some three decades ago, "we sent the Army to Vietnam to save Vietnam; we withdrew the Army to save the Army." The same is even more true for Iraq today. . . .

The Army Is Misusing the Troops

Today there is little doubt that the ground forces are overstretched. In early March, [2007] we at the Center for American Progress released a study chronicling the effects that sustained deployments in Iraq are having on the Army. By analyzing every Army brigade we were able to convey the strain and fatigue placed on the force and illustrate its implications for our nation's national security. The facts that we compiled are troubling:

> Of the Army's 44 combat brigades, all but the First Brigade of the Second Infantry Division, which is permanently based in South Korea, have served at least one tour. Of the remaining 43:
>
> —12 Brigades have had one tour in Iraq or Afghanistan
>
> —20 Brigades have had two tours in Iraq or Afghanistan

Many Military Jobs Are Already Overstaffed

A draft would do nothing to help the Defense Department solve its more serious military personnel problems. Indeed, the biggest problem the department faces is not that it lacks people, but that it has the wrong people for many of its jobs.

In recent years, the services were overstaffed in about 40 percent of their occupations, even as they suffered shortages in about 30 percent. True, the Army is short of infantry and military police, but it has temporary authority to increase its ranks by 30,000 troops. By contrast, the Air Force is overstaffed by 24,000 members and the Navy wants to thin its ranks by 25,000 sailors. Both the Navy and the Air Force are short-staffed in critical skills such as electronic systems repair and some information, specialties, and they have too many people in mundane occupations.

Cindy Williams, "Forget the Draft," Advice+Dissent, Govexec.com, September 15, 2004, www.comw.org/qdr/fulltext/0409williams.pdf.

—9 Brigades have had three tours in Iraq or Afghanistan

—2 Brigades have had four tours in Iraq or Afghanistan

Additionally, the task of sustaining or increasing troop levels in Iraq has forced the Army to frequently violate its own deployment policy. Army policy holds that after 12 months of deployment in a combat zone, troops should receive 24 months at home for recuperation and retraining before returning to combat. Even before the surge, the Army had reduced dwell time to one year. Increasing troop levels in Iraq will only force the Army to place more strain on those serving. In fact, on April 2nd [2007] the Pentagon announced that two units will be sent back to Iraq without even a year at home. Extending deployments and shortening dwell time cause havoc on the lives of those serving in uniform.

The Army Is Failing to Recruit and Train Volunteers

It is also wrong, both militarily and morally, to send troops into a war zone who are not fully combat ready. Three units that are part of this surge show what happens when units do not receive what the Army calls the proper dwell time between deployments.

- The 1st Brigade of the Army's 3rd Infantry Division based at Fort Stewart became the Army's first brigade to be deployed to Iraq for the third time. It was sent over in January 2007 after about a year at home. But because of its compressed time between deployments, some 150 soldiers joined the unit right out of basic training, too late to participate in the training necessary to prepare soldiers to function effectively in Iraq. Unfortunately one of the 18-year-old soldiers, Matthew Zeimer, who joined the unit on Dec. 18, 2006, was killed on Feb. 2nd after being at his first combat post for just two hours. He missed the brigade's intensive four-week pre-Iraq training at the national training center at Fort Irwin, California, getting instead a cut rate 10-day course.

- The 4th Brigade of the Army's 1st Infantry Division based at Fort Reilly was sent to Iraq in February [2007] about a year after it was reactivated. More than half of the brigade's soldiers classified as E-4 or below and are right out of basic training and the bulk of its mid-level non-commissioned officers in the ranks of E-5 and E-6 have no combat experience.

- The 3rd Division's 3rd Brigade was sent back to Iraq [in April 2007] for the third time after spending less than 11 months at home. In order to meet personnel requirements the brigade sent some 75 soldiers with medical problems into the war zone. These include troops with serious injuries and other medical problems, including GIs who doctors have said are medically unfit for battle. Medical records show that some are too injured to wear their body armor. According to Steve Robinson of Veterans for America, "this smacks of an overstretched military that is in crisis mode to get people onto the battlefield."

The strain on personnel and the difficulty of recruiting new soldiers in the midst of an unpopular war has prompted the Army to relax many of its standards and dramatically increase enlistment and recruitment bonuses.

While overall retention is good, the Army is keeping its numbers up by increasing financial incentives and allowing soldiers to reenlist early. Worryingly, however, retention among West Point graduates is declining and the Army's personnel costs continue to increase. Spending on enlistment and recruitment bonuses tripled from $328 million before the war in Iraq to over $1 billion in 2006. The incentives for Army Guard and Reserve have grown ten-fold over the same period.

After failing to meet its recruitment target for 2005, the Army raised the maximum age for enlistment from 35 to 40 in January—only to find it necessary to raise it to 42 in June. Basic training, an essential tool for developing and training new recruits, has increasingly become a rubber-stamping ritual. Through the first six months of 2006, only 7.6 percent of new recruits failed basic training, down from 18.1 percent in May 2005.

Alarmingly, this drop in boot-camp attrition coincides with a lowering of recruitment standards. The number of

Army recruits who scored below average on its aptitude test doubled in 2005, and the Army has doubled the number of non-high school graduates it enlisted last year. In 2006, only 81 percent of the new enlistees have high school diplomas, compared to 94 percent before the invasion. Even as more allowances are made, the Government Accountability Office reported that allegations and substantiated claims of recruiter wrongdoing have increased by 50 percent. [In May 2006], for example, the Army signed up an autistic man to become a cavalry scout. . . .

Expanding and Rebuilding the Ground Forces

Secretary Gates' decision to expand the Army and Marines is long overdue. At the Center for American Progress we have been calling for such an expansion for the past four years. However, the difficult situation facing the Army and the Marines requires a long-term approach toward expanding and rebuilding the ground forces. Increasing the size of the Army and Marines will not help the situation on the ground in Iraq. Instead, growing these forces is about preparing America's military for the future. I have the following recommendations:

Don't Lower Standards. The Army and Marines should meet their new end-strength goals without relaxing recruitment standards or retention and promotion criteria. In order to ensure the Army and Marines continue to get the best and the brightest, the current target of adding 7,000 soldiers and 5,000 marines per year is too ambitious in light of current circumstances and should be scaled back. Recruitment and retention standards should return to at least pre-Iraq standards. Congress must make sure that the quality of U.S. military personnel does not slide as it did in the 1970s. It is worth waiting a few extra years to ensure that the Army and Marines attract the men and women who possess the specialized skill sets needed for an effective 21st-century military.

Expand with a Focus on Peacekeeping and Counterinsurgency Operations. Following the war in Vietnam, instead of building off the experience of fighting an unconventional force, the military adopted the mantra of "no more Vietnams" and shifted its focus back to confronting conventional threats. We cannot make this same mistake today. It is clear going forward that America's ground forces have to be prepared to engage an entire spectrum of operations, from conventional ground combat to humanitarian and peacekeeping operations. The wars in Iraq and Afghanistan have shown that while our ground forces remain conventionally unmatched, there is significant room for improvement in our ability to conduct counterinsurgency and peacekeeping operations. In my view, the U.S. Army should consider developing specialized "peacekeeping" or "stabilization and reconstruction" brigades. Such specialized brigades would alter both the type of recruit the Army is seeking and the type of person who might be interested in joining the Army. It is important, therefore, that the decision about whether to create specialized brigades of this sort be made as soon as possible.

Grow the Forces in a Fiscally Responsible Manner. Growing the ground forces is an expensive endeavor. The current average annual cost of maintaining a single service member already exceeds $100,000. Currently the defense budget is severely unbalanced. Despite claims that 9/11 changed everything, during Secretary Rumsfeld's tenure only two weapons systems were canceled. Many of the current weapons programs are unnecessary relics that were borne out of Cold War-era thinking. The challenge confronting the Army and Marines in terms of both escalating personnel costs and the deepening equipment crisis requires significant congressional attention and funding. Expanding the ground forces and recovering from Iraq and Afghanistan should be the overriding priority of the defense budget.

Open up the Military to all Americans who Possess the Desire, Talent and Character to Serve. The Army and Marine Corps cannot afford to place unnecessary obstacles in the way of qualified men and women who want to serve. To this end, the military should make two major changes to its personnel policy.

- First, repeal the "don't ask, don't tell" policy. The "don't ask, don't tell" policy is counterproductive to military readiness. Over the past 10 years more than 10,000 personnel have been discharged as a result of this policy, including 800 with skills deemed "mission critical," such as pilots, combat engineers, and linguists. These are the very job functions for which the military has experienced personnel shortfalls. General John M. Shalikashvili, the Chairman of the Joint Chiefs of Staff in 1993 when the "don't ask, don't tell" policy was enacted, no longer supports the policy on the grounds that allowing gay men and women to serve openly in the military would no longer create intolerable tension among personnel and undermine cohesion. Additionally, a recent Zogby poll supports this view. It found that three-quarters of Afghanistan and Iraq veterans were comfortable interacting with gay people.

- Second, all military occupations should be open to whoever qualifies, regardless of gender. Currently, the Army prohibits women from serving in infantry, field artillery, and Special Forces units that directly engage the enemy on the ground. The idea that women who possess the requisite mental and physical skills should somehow be "protected" from the dangers of combat fails to acknowledge the reality of the modern battlefield and the role women are already playing in Iraq and Afghanistan. Nearly a hundred women have been killed in these wars. We only impede our ability to build a 21st-century military by constructing barriers where none need exist.

> "The other advantage of a draft was that it is far cheaper than a volunteer military. Supporters of the volunteer force concede building up a larger force is costly."

A Draft Is Cheaper Than Financing the All-Volunteer Military

Julian E. Barnes and Peter Spiegel

In the following viewpoint, Los Angeles Times staff writers Julian E. Barnes and Peter Spiegel describe problems with Bush administration proposals to expand the U.S. armed forces without reinstituting the draft. Meeting current recruiting goals not only means lowering educational standards and raising recruitment age, Barnes and Spiegel report, but also means huge spending increases for enlistment bonuses, marketing campaigns, and more recruiters' salaries. Rep. Charles B. Rangel (D-NY) and military sociologist Charles Moskos are among those who advocate a return to the draft because it is both cheaper and fairer—as it is, they say, the burden of fighting falls disproportionately on the working class, who have fewer options and need the enlistment bonuses more.

Julian E. Barnes and Peter Spiegel, "Expanding the Military, Without a Draft," *Los Angeles Times*, December 24, 2006. Reproduced by permission of the publisher and author.

As you read, consider the following questions:

1. How many new recruits did the army seek in 2006, according to the authors?

2. According to Barnes and Spiegel, how much does the army pay in bonuses to enlistees who sign up for four years or more of active duty? How much for a six-year commitment in the reserves?

3. How much does the Congressional Budget Office estimate must be spent on enlistment bonuses to increase the number of enlistees by 6,500 per year, according to the authors?

President [George W.] Bush's call to build up the size of the Army and Marine Corps confronts the U.S. military with a sizable and potentially costly challenge, especially given its recent history of war-related recruiting problems. But one solution remains firmly off the table: reinstituting a draft.

Bush in December 2006 endorsed proposals to increase the size of the two services. The proposals have wide support, from those who advocate a short-term boost in the number of troops in Iraq as well as those who say a larger overall force will be needed even if troops are moved out of Iraq.

By boosting incentives and bonus money, adding recruiters and continuing to increase the military advertising budget, the Army should be able to sign up an additional 10,000 people a year within the current [2006] all-volunteer system, according to many military experts. But they add that such an increase would be costly. An additional 10,000 soldiers would cost at least an additional $1.2 billion annually.

"We've been at it for 30-plus years," said Theodore G. Stroup Jr., a retired lieutenant general and former head of the Army personnel system. "We do not want to go back to a draft."

Lowered Recruitment Standards Cost Professional and Equity Services

Supporters of the volunteer force say it is of much higher quality than that of the draft era, which ended in 1973. But critics suggest the Army already has lowered its standards to meet current recruiting goals and would have to lower them even more to meet a larger goal.

Since the beginning of the Iraq war, the number of recruits with high school diplomas has fallen sharply, according to a new study by the National Priorities Project, a research group in Massachusetts. The number of soldiers with a general equivalency diploma—as opposed to a high school diploma—rose from 13.1% in 2004 to 26.7% in 2006, according to the study, based on Army documents obtained through a Freedom of Information request.

"Someone holding a regular high school diploma may still have more options than someone holding some alternative credential," said Anita Dancs, the research director for the priorities project.

Current and former defense officials deny that changes in recruitment standards have adversely affected quality.

"The quality of the force is outstanding," said Bernard Rostker, a former undersecretary of Defense and onetime head of the Selective Service system. "There are plenty of people who we don't take today who are quite adequate to do the jobs we need."

Although top generals were reluctant to give up the draft in the 1970s and move to the all-volunteer force, most in the military today believe that a reinstatement of conscription would reduce the professionalism and experience of the force.

The Iraq war is the longest the all-volunteer Army has had to fight, and the demands of the yearlong rotations in and out of Iraq are straining the military and its sprawling recruiting system.

Bush voiced support for calls to increase the size of the Army and Marines but did not specify how large an increase he wanted over the 507,000 now serving. The Assn. of the U.S. Army, the service's influential advocacy group, has proposed an increase of 100,000. Other proposals call for increases of 20,000 to 30,000.

After struggling in 2004, the Army missed its recruiting target in 2005. To meet its recruiting goal of 80,000 new soldiers in 2006, the Army was forced to loosen rules for those they were willing to accept. Commanders have allowed an increase in the number of "Category 4" recruits, enlistees who score the lowest on military aptitude tests, and have raised the enlistment age from 35 to 42.

According to Army data, the service also has issued more than 13,600 medical or "moral character" waivers to recruits in 2006, up more than 2,500 over last year's levels. Waivers given to recruits who had been engaged in "serious misconduct" in the past—crimes, repeated instances of substance abuse or misconduct involving weapons—nearly doubled, from 630 to 1,017, and those for recruits with misdemeanors on their records went from 4,587 to 6,542.

As recruiting problems have grown, so has the economic disparity within the military. According to the National Priorities Project, the number of recruits from wealthy neighborhoods continues to decline. Although wealthy ZIP codes have long been underrepresented in the armed forces, the numbers dropped further from 2004 to 2006, said Dancs, the group's research director.

"They are having a difficult time signing up recruits into the armed forces, and that does seem to be tied to the unpopularity of the Iraq war," she said. "Our data shows those with more options pursue other options." . . .

Benefits of the Draft

Rep. Charles B. Rangel (D-N.Y.), incoming chairman of the tax-writing House Ways and Means Committee, has proposed

Mandatory National Service Would Be Far Cheaper than the All-Volunteer Military

The economic costs of universal national service would not be exorbitant.

[Communitarian scholar Amitai] Etzioni estimates that if every 18-year-old participated, total cost would be $33 billion a year ($11,000 per person times three million people). [Analyst Steven] Waldman [estimates] $12,000 per person per year—but even that works out to only $36 billion per year, about one-ninth the military budget.

And that's not counting deductions for, e.g., salaries for young people who'd be in the military anyway; savings on welfare and unemployment; and savings from reduction in crime.

Indirect economic gains might be even greater. Etzioni points to some of them when he says, "By encouraging and developing the virtues of hard work, responsibility and co-operation—to name a few—national service would . . . improve economic productivity. [And it] would probably provide young people with greater maturity and skills than they would normally have upon entering college or vocational training[, further] benefiting themselves and the community."

Mark Satin,
"Bring Back the Draft—for Everyone!—and Offer Community and *Military Options,"* Radical Middle Newsletter, *March 2002.*

reinstitution of the draft in part to address disparity concerns. And Veterans Affairs Secretary Jim Nicholson, a Vietnam War veteran, said Thursday [December 21, 2006] that he thought "society would benefit" from a draft. Nicholson later issued a statement to say that he did not support reinstitution of the draft.

Charles Moskos, a military sociologist and professor emeritus at Northwestern University, said that without a draft, the burden of war falls disproportionately on the working class. He noted that of his 1956 Princeton University class of 750 men, 450 served. In the Princeton University class of 2006 there were 1,108 men and women, but only nine so far have joined the military.

"They call this an all-volunteer military," Moskos said. "But in the United States we are paying people to die for us."

Moskos said the other advantage of a draft was that it is far cheaper than a volunteer military. Supporters of the volunteer force concede building up a larger force is costly.

"I think it is going to be very expensive," said Sen. Jack Reed (D-R.I.). "But you cannot avoid it. We have a situation now where we do not have a strategic reserve. . . . This is no longer a nice thing, this has become essential."

After missing 2005 recruiting goals, the Army sharply increased bonuses offered to those willing to sign up for extended tours. In January [2006] the maximum for a recruit enlisting for four years or more in the active-duty Army was doubled from $20,000 to $40,000. Six-year commitments for the reserves went from $10,000 to $20,000.

The Army in October also unveiled a new marketing campaign aimed at recruits, called "Army Strong," which will cost the service $200 million every year.

The incentives have borne fruit. The 2006 recruiting season, which ended in October, saw the Army pull in 80,635 recruits, just over its 80,000 goal. It has stayed above targets since then [as of December 2006].

But it may not be the most cost-effective approach. A Congressional Budget Office study released in October found that adding more recruiters on the ground generated more enlistees, and frequently cost less, than national ad campaigns and increased bonuses.

The CBO said an additional 800 to 1,100 recruiters, which would cost up to $150 million every year, could increase the number of enlistees annually by 6,500 to eventually reach new targets. By relying on enlistment bonuses, on the other hand, the costs would run as high as $430 million.

The CBO warned, however, that adding 15,000 to 20,000 soldiers by 2010 would take recruitment and retention rates that had never been sustained over long periods.

"Whether the Army components will be able to increase their forces to authorized end-strength levels is an open question," the CBO warned.

Reed said that because of the recruiting problems, and the ongoing war, the growth of the military would have to be incremental. "It will be a real struggle for many, many reasons," Reed said. "It is hard to recruit now given the story is all abut Iraq, about the conflict there, casualties there."

But Reed, a former Army officer, said the challenges were worth tackling to avoid the problems of a draft and the division it creates in the country.

"They are getting people who want to be there," Reed said. "It's a lot different than someone saying, 'I am here against my will.'"

> *"The draft does not cut the cost of military preparedness. If anything, it increases the cost and discourages efficient resource use."*

A Draft Is More Costly Than Financing the All-Volunteer Army

John C. Goodman

John C. Goodman is the president of the National Center for Policy Analysis, a nonprofit public policy research institute in Washington, D.C., that seeks private-sector alternatives to government regulation in such areas as taxation, Social Security, the environment, and health care. In the following viewpoint, Goodman examines the military draft from an economic perspective and finds that conscription is far more costly to society than the all-voluntary military that now serves the United States. Volunteers and draftees alike are not producing civilian goods and services when they perform a military job, Goodman argues. These costs and taxes are hard to quantify but they exist, he says, and taxpayers and draftees shoulder them even when the military pays draftees less than it has to pay volunteers. Moreover, he

John C. Goodman, "The Economic Cost of Drafted Labor," *National Center for Policy Analysis Debate Central*, 2006. Copyright © 2006 National Center for Policy Analysis. All rights reserved. Reproduced by permission.

contends, draftees reenlist less often so training costs are higher, and during a draft era many civilians would undertake costly draft-avoidance measures that must be factored in as well. Goodman also considers the draft unfair to the poor and a violation of citizens' freedom of conscience, which he calls implicit taxes on society that are not imposed by the all-volunteer military.

As you read, consider the following questions:

1. What are "opportunity costs," in Goodman's definition?
2. According to Goodman, what did a Vietnam-era commission conclude was the dollar burden on the general public for every dollar that conscription cost draftees?
3. How do pro-draft groups such as professional military officers, defense industries, and agricultural interests benefit financially from the draft, in the author's view?

The issue of cost is central to the debate over drafted labor versus volunteer labor. To an economist, the cost of doing anything is measured in terms of the value of other opportunities that must be foregone in order to do that thing. The cost of buying a steak for dinner is measured in terms of passing up the opportunity to spend the same money on chicken, fish, a movie or a haircut. The cost of studying for an economics exam is the loss of the opportunity to spend the time sleeping or studying chemistry. Similarly, but on a larger scale, the cost of maintaining an army is properly measured by the foregone opportunities to put the same labor and capital to work producing other valuable goods and services. Economists refer to costs expressed in terms of foregone opportunities as opportunity costs. . . .

How can we place a dollar value on the cost of moving one person from a civilian to a military job? As a starting point, we could use that person's civilian wage or salary, which, let's say, is $20,000 a year. In a market economy, workers in the private sector are usually paid according to what they produce. No employer can make a profit by paying a worker $20,000 a year unless the worker adds at least that much to the firm's output. At the same time, competition among employers assures that such a worker will not have to settle for a job that pays much less than a $20,000. So $20,000 a year would be an adequate guess at the opportunity cost of moving $20,000-a-year worker from a civilian to a military job.

To get a more refined estimate of opportunity cost, other factors would have to be considered. First, the civilian job might give the worker a little more (or a little less) valuable on-the-job training than does the military job. In addition, life in the army might be a little more (or a little less) hazardous, boring or unpleasant than civilian life. Since the category "other goods and services" includes such intangibles as on-the-job training, security and peace of mind, we must adjust the original figure of $20,000 to take these into account.

All things considered, most economists would say that the best estimate of the opportunity cost of shifting a person from a civilian to a military job is the minimum amount that person would have to be paid to take the military job voluntarily. If it would take a $25,000 inducement to shift our $20,000 civilian worker to the military voluntarily, then the opportunity cost of making the shift is that $25,000.

It is important to understand that the same opportunity cost must be borne regardless of whether people are shifted from civilian to military life by the draft or by a payment large enough to induce them to volunteer. The primary effect of using draftees rather than volunteers is not to reduce the cost of military preparedness, but simply to shift the cost. If our subject were offered $25,000 a year, and enlisted voluntarily, he would end up no worse off than in civilian life. In this case, the entire burden of the increase in military preparedness falls on the general taxpayer. If the same person is drafted and paid only $15,000 a year, the burden on the general taxpayer is reduced, but the draftee bears an implicit annual tax of $10,000. This implicit tax is equal to the difference between the pay of a draftee and the pay of a volunteer. The total burden is the same in both cases; the draft simply shifts that burden.

The Draft Increases the Burden of Military Preparedness

What we have said is at least true as a first approximation. Further examination of the matter suggests that the draft may actually increase the burden of military preparedness at the same time it shifts it. Why the increase?

- Draftees tend to reenlist less often than volunteers; this in turn tends to lower productivity and raise training costs.

- Morale tends to be lower in an army of draftees.

- Military commanders, thinking of draftees as "cheap" manpower, may use them wastefully, disregarding their personal skills or the possibility of substituting hardware for personnel.

- Finally, a draft induces many civilians to undertake costly draft-avoidance measures, such as choosing a draft-exempt but otherwise unattractive career, retaining expensive legal counsel or even spending years in jail or exile.

Many of these costs are intangible and hard to measure. Nonetheless, there has been at least one attempt to estimate them. A presidential commission established near the end of the Vietnam War concluded that for each $1.00 of implicit tax collected from draftees, a burden of approximately $2.50 was placed on the general public. That suggests that the implicit tax of the draft is far more expensive to levy than the explicit taxes used to finance a volunteer army.

Evaluating the Draft

This analysis of the economic effects of conscription gives us a basis on which to evaluate proposals to abandon the volunteer army and reestablish a draft. Some critics condemn the volunteer army as unfair and excessively costly. How do their arguments stand up? We will evaluate the draft according to three values many people hold: (1) efficiency, (2) fairness to the least well off and (3) liberty.

Efficiency. Let's begin with efficiency. Generally, achieving a goal efficiently means achieving it at minimum cost. This means minimizing the sacrifice required to achieve the goal. It is true that the budgetary cost of a drafted army is lower than the budgetary cost of a volunteer army: With a drafted army the government pays less. But the budgetary cost is not the only cost: When all of the costs are considered, evidence strongly suggests that the volunteer approach is the less costly one. . . .

Fairness to the Least Well Off. Let's turn now to another standard of evaluation. How should we judge the draft as compared with a volunteer army in terms of how each affects the most disadvantaged members of the community? This standard of evaluation has figured prominently in the debate and deserves careful attention.

Curiously enough, both the draft (during the Vietnam era) and the volunteer army (at present) have been attacked as being unfair to the poor—and to poor minorities in particular. Youths from poverty-level backgrounds, including many minority youths, have been heavily overrepresented in the lowest military ranks under both systems. This has been among the factors leading Senator Edward Kennedy and others to favor a

Draft Supporters Underestimate the Cost of Conscription

Some argue that depending on an all-volunteer military is too expensive. That's wrong. The true cost of having a man in the military is what society has to forgo, what economists call opportunity costs. Say a man worked producing televisions for which he was paid $1,000 a month. If he's drafted, he's not producing $1,000 worth of televisions. The sacrificed $1,000 worth of televisions is part of the cost of his being in the military whether he's paid $68 a month or nothing a month.

Walter Williams, "Reinstating the Military Draft,"
Capitalism Magazine, *December 28, 2006.*

truly universal national service that would draw forces proportionately from all segments of the community because no one would be exempt.

Before accepting this solution to the problem, however, we need to understand more clearly the nature of the problem itself. The overrepresentation of poor and minority youth in the military actually has very different implications under a volunteer system than under a draft.

Under the draft each conscript bears the burden of a large implicit tax; having shouldered this burden the draftee then performs defense services for all citizens. If most draftees are drawn from lower-income groups, then the draft acts as a mechanism for transferring income and wealth from the poor to everyone else, including the middle class and the rich.

Under a volunteer army things are quite different. Volunteers are fully compensated for defense services they render. If a person feels that the compensation is inadequate, he or she simply need not volunteer. We can expect that some volunteers will be paid the bare minimum necessary to compensate them for giving up civilian life. But for a person whose civilian opportunities are meager, joining the army might lead to a significant boost in income. The lower the volunteer's civilian income, the greater the net benefit of joining the army. If the poor are overrepresented in a volunteer army, the volunteer army is probably working to transfer income and wealth from the general taxpayer to the poor.

Liberty. How do the draft and volunteer army rate in terms of protecting the rights and liberties of individual citizens? Answers to this question vary according to one's conception of just what rights and liberties are important to protect. Let's consider three possibilities.

First, there is a strongly ingrained American tradition that freedom of conscience and religion are among the most important of all individual rights. A draft that did not respect religious belief would be opposed even by many who favored a draft on other grounds. By treating conscientious objectors according to special rules, our Selective Service System has at least partially recognized the force of this argument.

Second, some oppose the draft on much broader grounds than simple freedom of conscience: Many Americans honor a tradition of self-defense under which each person has a right to defend his own person and property and has no right to impose that responsibility on others. In Revolutionary War times, self-defense meant keeping a rifle beside your plough; in modern times, it means either volunteering for military service yourself or accepting the responsibility of paying someone else to provide defense services for you. A tax-supported volunteer army is thus reasonably consistent with the self-defense tradition; the draft is not.

Finally, we ought to take note of an almost opposite tradition that imposes a duty on young men to defend their community and that grants a right to all others so to be defended. This tradition is much older than the self-defense tradition— older, in fact, than Western civilization itself. Even in the 20th century, there have been those who believe it to be not simply expedient but just and proper that young men bear a disproportionate share of the defense burden through the draft. President Dwight D. Eisenhower, for example, favored universal national service as much on moral grounds as he did for the value of services it produced. "If the program accomplished nothing more," he wrote, "than to produce cleanliness and decent grooming, it might be worth the price tag."

The Political Economy of the Draft

Let's take a moment to summarize. The draft does not cut the cost of military preparedness. If anything, it increases the cost and discourages efficient resource use. As it has worked in the past, the draft has transferred income from the poor to the rich, while our present volunteer army transfers income from the rich to the poor. And many people consider the draft offensive to individual rights and liberties. Why, then, is the idea of a draft always being revived?. . .

Draftees are a minority. In fact, until the voting age was lowered they were a disenfranchised minority. How convenient for everyone else to ask them to foot a disproportionate part of the bill for military preparedness!

Of course, our political system is not a perfect direct democracy. In a representative system, special-interest groups often wield political power that is out of proportion to the numerical voting strength of those groups. In particular, groups that are compact, that regularly communicate with each other through their daily activities, and that share easily identified common interests tend to be proportionately more politically powerful than groups that are large, scattered and diffuse. Potential draftees normally have not constituted an effective pressure group—although when the draft began to threaten college students during the Vietnam War, they at least briefly became one. On the other side, certain prodraft groups have long enjoyed significant political influence. Among these are:

- Professional military officers. Although the draft does not cut the opportunity cost of military preparedness, it does significantly cut the labor supply budgetary cost. That leaves more dollars in the budget for sophisticated hardware, weapons research and military retirement benefits.

- Defense industries. When people are drafted during a conflict, civilian labor supply is reduced and wages increase. If defense jobs carry draft exemptions (as has often been the case), however, defense industries are insulated from this upward pressure on costs, resulting in more profits for arms makers.

- The agricultural establishment. Like defense jobs, farm jobs have always carried deferments. By enhancing the supply of farm workers, the draft subsidizes farm labor costs. Until the draft was discontinued in 1971, the law even contained a provision that farm deferments would continue even when there were agricultural surpluses. . . .

For the time being, the political balance favors a volunteer army. Nonetheless, the national debate on the issues continues. If proposals for universal national service were ever to win out, conscription might be instituted on a wider scale than ever before. We can only hope that before any sweeping programs are instituted they are subjected to careful and informed consideration.

> *"The Army's Stop-Loss program, initi-*
> *ated in November 2002, allows it to in-*
> *definitely extend the term of active duty*
> *soldiers past their scheduled release*
> *date."*

The Army's Stop-Loss Policy Is a "Back-Door" Draft

Christopher Hayes

Christopher Hayes is a senior editor of In These Times, *a maga-zine of investigative journalism, politics, culture, and progressive opinion. In the following viewpoint, Hayes claims that the U.S. military, well aware of public opposition to reinstituting the draft, is quietly drafting people anyway by extending soldiers' tours of duty beyond their enlistment period, without their con-sent. Hayes reports more than 800 cases of this "backdoor draft" occurred in December 2005, returning reservists to active-duty status and then to combat duty in Iraq, even after the army bowed to public pressure and officially announced the end of this practice a month earlier. Soldiers with only weeks left to the end of their service contract, many of whom have already served in*

Afghanistan and Iraq, are understandably resentful, says Hayes, but fear reprisal as long as they are not officially discharged and rarely protest.

As you read, consider the following questions:

1. What is the IRR, and what is the difference between the current call-up and the only other mobilization of its members during the first Gulf War, according to Hayes?

2. How many of the 7,380 IRR members who received mobilization orders have formally filed for exemptions or simply not shown up, according to the author?

3. Why does Hayes suggest the army is forced to conduct the backdoor draft?

For more than 800 members of the Army's Individual Ready Reserve (IRR), the most memorable part of the 2005 holiday season was a surprise stocking-stuffer from the United States Army. It came in the form of a blue and white Western Union Mailgram that ordered them to report for active duty in Operation Iraqi Freedom.

Eric, a second-year law student, who completed four years of active duty in 2002, was at his parents' house on Christmas Eve when they handed him what looked like an innocuous piece of mail from the Secretary of the Army. "I was pretty shocked," Eric (not his real name) says. "I went up to my room and hyperventilated for a bit and then came back down and didn't tell anyone for two days. I didn't want to ruin Christmas."

The Backdoor Draft Is Still Occurring

You might remember this practice by the name critics gave it during the 2004 presidential election: the "backdoor draft." In June of that year, the Pentagon announced the initial call-ups of the IRR [Individual Ready Reserve]—a rarely-deployed group of about 114,000 soldiers who have completed their active duty requirements and returned to civilian life. This raised the specter of soldiers being pulled back into military service against their will, generating headlines, controversy and uncomfortable memories of Vietnam. It also proved to be such a headache to administer that in November 2005 the Army appeared to capitulate to pressure by suspending the program. But as *In These Times* learned, the program has not been suspended. In exclusive interviews, six soldiers who received mobilization orders expressed anger and frustration about what they say is a bad-faith effort by the Army to wring extra service out of those who are about to complete their service commitment. Nearly all asked that their names be changed in this article for fear of reprisal as they negotiate their responses to these orders.

"Back when people started using the phrase 'backdoor draft,' I was really skeptical," says one ex-ROTC cadet, who strongly opposes the Iraq war. "Now that I've been served papers, it really does feel like that."

All of the officers interviewed who received orders to deploy in late December have one thing in common: They all started active duty in 1998, which means their full 8-year contract with the Army—or Mandatory Service Obligation (MSO)—will expire in May [2006]. "We're all coming up on our MSO dates," says Jason, who along with about 40 other members of West Point's Class of 1998 received a call-up. "I get the impression that they did a check to see who they were coming close to losing and went ahead and sent out the orders." Army spokeswoman Lt. Col. Pamela Hart denied this, insisting that "no population was singled out."

With only four months left before being officially discharged, Jason and others now face an 18-month tour of active duty in Iraq. "The Army is using two different rules for their benefit," says Paul Trotter, an ex-ROTC cadet who has already served in both Afghanistan and Iraq. "They've got one rule that says we can call you up from the IRR at any point before your obligation is done. They've got another rule that says once you're on active duty, we can Stop-Loss you so you have to stay." The Army's Stop-Loss program, initiated in November 2002, allows it to indefinitely extend the term of active duty soldiers past their scheduled release date.

That means that for thousands of soldiers, the contract they signed pledging 8 years of service no longer holds any weight. In January 2004, Defense Secretary Donald Rumsfeld signed an authorization for involuntary mobilization. The IRR was last called up was during the first Gulf War. But then, soldiers were deployed to backfill Army positions in Germany and other bases rather than deployed directly into the combat theater. "When I was in the army, it was clear that if you're in the IRR, the only time you're going to go off to war is World War III," says Kevin O'Meara, a 43-year-old former Army human resources officer. O'Meara received a mobilization order in 2004 from which he was subsequently exempted. "The IRR was not designed for what was supposed to be this little jaunt in the desert."

"When I signed my contract, the impression was that the IRR was rarely used, only in a national emergency," says Jason. "I didn't think it would be used as a manpower tool to support an occupation."

Enforcement Is Difficult

From the moment the IRR call-up was announced in the summer of 2004, the Army had a difficult time enforcing its order. The Army was forced to abandon attempts to mobilize thousands of officers who had completed their 8-year commitment but hadn't sent in the paperwork to remove their names from the IRR rolls. As of December 11, 2005, of the 7,380 soldiers who received orders to mobilize, 3,521 have filed for exemptions or delays and nearly 500 have simply not shown up.

Stop Loss Is Unconstitutional

Some people question the legality of the Stop Loss policy on the grounds that it violates the Constitutional prohibition on "involuntary servitude." This presents the Department of Defense with a dilemma, because the longstanding precedent for exception to the 13th Amendment is the draft. So by precedent, the 13th Amendment has already been violated repeatedly since it was first enacted every time the country needed to fill its ranks with cannon fodder. The dilemma now is that the administration does not want to use this particular precedent to justify Stop Loss, because the regime is denying that the policy is—as many critics have called it—a back door draft. This is not a legal show-stopper for Stop Loss, but certainly an embarrassment for people who don't want to use the D-word.

Stan Goff, "Back-Door Law, Back-Door Draft,"
FromTheWilderness.com, *May 25, 2005.*

On November 18, 2005, the *Washington Post* reported that the Army was throwing in the towel. The Army has "suspended plans to expand an unwieldy, 16-month-old program to call up inactive soldiers for military duty," the *Post* reported, "after thousands have requested delays or exemptions or failed to show up."

For many soldiers, this meant they were off the hook. "I felt relieved after that *Washington Post* article," says Jason, the West Point grad. "Then on the 20th of December, I get the mailgram."

Lt. Col. Hart says that the December mobilization orders are all part of the original involuntary mobilization authorized in 2004 and that the Army will continue to issue such orders until it has successfully deployed 5,600 active-duty soldiers from the ranks of the IRR. So far, nearly 4,000 have deployed.

"We have 114,000 soldiers in the IRR and we're only looking at 7,000 who've received orders," Hart says. "Now mind you, it can be traumatic for the individual solider, but looking at the big picture it's understandable."

The news of the orders quickly spread among soldiers, as many scrambled to figure out their options. O'Meara, who has covered the issue on his blog, the Command T.O.C., says nearly two dozen soldiers have contacted him, seeking advice on how to file for exemptions. Most exemptions, he says, are initially denied, but many succeed on appeal. So far, the Army has issued 1,616 of them. Every soldier interviewed for this article said they intend to file for an exemption based on health, family or schooling circumstances.

What frustrates these soldiers the most is a sense that the Army isn't being straight with them. "Back in July in '04 when I left active duty, if they'd said 'You can't leave, you have to do another tour,' I wouldn't have been happy about it," says Paul Trotter, who is seeking an exemption so he can continue to help home-school his autistic, seven-year-old son. "But I'd have much rather done that than have a life set up and a job and moved and all that stuff and then be told pull chocks out of that and go back to Iraq."

More confounding, each soldier had received phone calls and/or emails shortly before their mailgrams asking if they'd like to volunteer for the same deployment to which they've since been ordered. "I want to emphasize that we are only establishing a volunteer roster at this time," wrote an Army Career Management officer in an email to Jason two weeks before he received his mailgram.

The day after receiving his orders, Jason called the Career officer thinking there had been some mistake. "She said she was kind of upset with the way it had been handled," he says. "It turns out they had intended all along to call up everyone they contacted. It was never going to be voluntary."

Fear of Reprisal Stifles Objections

The Army's effort to pull soldiers into active duty service just a few months before their contracts expire suggests that despite talk of draw-downs, military leaders anticipate that Operation Iraqi Freedom will need every last body they can get for the foreseeable future.

"There's this lack of courage on the part of politicians to admit that they need more bodies to do this," Eric says. "If the Army started a general draft there'd be public outcry, but because they're targeting people in the military who fear reprisal, people stay quiet about it and try to deal with it on their own."

"The basis of this is not a national emergency," says one officer, who echoed the sentiments of the group. "What this is is poor personnel planning."

> "*Expiration of the enlistment agreement does not automatically . . . convert [a soldier] back into a civilian. Instead, the military must [discharge] him, and until it does so, he remains a soldier.*"

The Army's Stop-Loss Policy Is a Legal Extension of Voluntary Enlistment

Daniel C. Brown

A military enlistment document is very different from an employment contract, attorney Daniel C. Brown explains in the following viewpoint. When they sign up, enlistees voluntarily agree to obey all lawful orders and undertake obligations not required of civilians—crucially, they are informed that the terms of the agreement are not promises and that Congress may change or add to their obligations no matter what the enlistment agreement says. Therefore, Brown argues, Congress and the courts have upheld the right of the president and the military to extend tours of duty, indefinitely if necessary, without consent, until a soldier is officially discharged. This so-called stop loss program indeed involves sacrifice and hardship, he says, but this is not a

Daniel C. Brown, "Stop Loss: Illegal Conscription in America?" *American University Law Review*, vol. 54, August 2005, pp. 1598–1600, 1602, 1606–1608, 1616–1617, 1622–1623, 1629–1631. Reproduced by permission.

backdoor draft, not breach of contract, and not illegal. Daniel C. Brown holds a law degree from American University in Washington, DC, and served as senior staff member at the American University Law Review.

As you read, consider the following questions:

1. On what grounds do Pentagon officials justify the stop loss program as it has been used during the war in Iraq, according to the author?
2. Under what three scenarios does the president have the power to extend the service of any member of the armed forces without his or her consent, according to Brown?
3. How does Brown suggest the army should better inform enlistees that unexpected, involuntary, indefinite active-duty service is part of their agreement?

The stop loss policy has undergone several changes in scope and application since it was implemented following the attacks of September 11, 2001, but all of its variations require designated enlisted soldiers to continue serving in the military beyond the expiration of their enlistment agreements and without their consent. Critics of stop loss frequently refer to it as the "backdoor draft," claiming that it effectively converts soldiers who enlisted voluntarily into conscripts once their agreements expire. Both Democratic and Republican politicians have criticized the policy, with Senators John Kerry and John McCain insisting the policy is a direct result of the Bush Administration's refusal to increase the size of the military and to deploy enough troops to Iraq. At a minimum, the much publicized reliance on stop loss is a sharp contradiction to the military's general emphasis on the concept of an "All Volunteer Force" ("AVF") as essential to its success.

Why Stop Loss Is Necessary

Pentagon officials insist that stop loss is necessary to promote and preserve unit cohesion. Pointing to lessons learned in Vietnam, they worry that the trust and effectiveness established among soldiers who have long trained and fought together in the same unit would erode if individual soldiers could leave as their enlistment terms ended. Normal attrition rates would cause a typical division to change out as many as 4,000 soldiers, about one-fifth of its total force, just before it deployed to a war zone. Officials argue that the prospect of soldiers in the same unit meeting for the first time on the battlefield would endanger their ability to work together effectively and would put their lives at risk. Stop loss also supports Army Chief of Staff General Peter Schoomaker's overall policy of rotating entire units—rather than individual soldiers—in and out of combat zones, which he asserts actually provides greater predictability to soldiers and their families.

Many observers contend, however, that even assuming that the maintenance of unit cohesion is a valid goal, the Army's heavy reliance on stop loss is explained by a much more fundamental problem: it simply has too few soldiers to handle major operations, such as those in Iraq and Afghanistan, while meeting other U.S. commitments around the world. Even if the Pentagon determined that rotating individual soldiers as their terms expire is not harmful to unit cohesion, the Army simply lacks the excess manpower to fill the vacancies that would arise without stop loss.

The President Has Stop-Loss Power

Although relevant statutes governing nonconsensual enlistment extensions appear facially contradictory, sensible interpretation and construction reveal that Congress intended to grant this power to the President in certain circumstances. While Congress could have been clearer, courts will find sufficient evidence to conclude that Congress intended to create exceptions on a case-by-case basis to the earlier bar on involuntary extensions made in lieu of congressional approval.

The presidential power to extend the enlistment of any member of the armed forces without the member's consent stems from 10 U.S.C. § 12,305. This power only arises when any member of the reserves has been ordered to active duty pursuant to one of three scenarios. . . . The three triggering scenarios consist of a war or national emergency declared by Congress, a national emergency declared by the President or the President's determination of a short-term necessity to reinforce active forces in an operational mission "other than during a war or national emergency." The President may then "suspend any provision of law related to promotion, retirement, or separation" of any member he deems essential to national security. President George W. Bush declared the requisite national emergency three days after the terrorist attacks of September 11, 2001 and delegated his authority to order reservists to active duty, thereby triggering the armed forces' ability to extend enlistments without the consent of enlistees. . . .

Stop Loss Does Not Violate the Enlistment Agreement

Nonconsensual extensions under stop loss arguably do not breach the enlistment agreement under contract law. A breach of contract is a failure to perform any binding promise that is part of the contract. The agreement document notifies enlistees that soldiers are subject to lawful orders and makes no representation that it summarizes all applicable laws nor any promise to enforce only those laws that are summarized in the document. In particular, it does not purport to list all circumstances under which a soldier's term of service may be extended. Therefore, while stop loss orders may be unexpected, courts are likely to find they do not breach any promise contained in the enlistment agreement. . . .

"'Indefinite' Means What It Says"

At the heart of the [stop loss] controversy is whether a law stating that commissioned reserve officers are appointed "for an indefinite term and are held during the pleasure of the President" gives the government the power to force them to serve permanently—as Army lawyers say—or only to discharge them against their will. . . .

Defense Department lawyers say that the federal law, including its use of the phrase "indefinite term," clearly gives the administration the authority to disapprove officer resignations. "The term 'indefinite' means what it says," they said . . . "An indefinite term has no specific length, but is rather unlimited."

Ann Scott Tyson,
"Army Using Policy to Deny Reserve Officer Resignations,"
washingtonpost.com, *May 11, 2006.*

Written in the first person, it states that the enlistee acknowledges and understands that the subsequent statements summarizing the law "*are not promises,*" that enlistment is "more than an employment agreement," that he is undertaking numerous obligations not required of civilians, that he must obey all lawful orders, that he will be subject to separation during or at the end of his enlistment, and that Congress may change or add to his obligations and benefits regardless of the content of the enlistment agreement. . . .

In deciding cases in which a breach of the enlistment agreement is alleged, courts frequently reproduce the language of *In re Grimley*. In that landmark case, decided in 1890, the Supreme Court went to great lengths to distinguish enlistment agreements from other types of contracts:

Enlistment is a contract, but it is one of those contracts which changes the status, and where that is changed, no breach of the contract destroys the new status or relieves from the obligations which its existence imposes. Marriage is a contract; but it is one which creates a status. Its contract obligations are mutual faithfulness; but a breach of those obligations does not destroy the status or change the relation of the parties to each other.

The government has at times argued that the Court's reasoning in *In re Grimley* meant that enlistees have no contractual rights in the traditional sense, and that the soldier's rights and obligations arise solely from statutes, leaving little room for courts to opine on contractual rights. Courts generally decline to accept such an extreme interpretation, which would carve out an area of contracts wholly outside their ability to review. But they do adopt the view that, by voluntarily assuming the status of soldier, enlistees acquire an all-or-nothing package of rights and obligations distinct from those of civilians. Furthermore, in contrast to private contractual arrangements, expiration of the enlistment agreement does not automatically release the soldier from his obligations and convert him back into a civilian. Instead, the military must undertake the affirmative act of discharging him, and until it does so, he remains a soldier. No breach will relieve him of his obligations as a soldier unless a court orders his discharge. And since enlistment contracts are not treated in the same manner as contracts between private parties, courts will not order the soldier's discharge simply because lawful orders given him are inconsistent with the terms of the agreement....

The Military Owes Enlistees Full Disclosure

Few would argue that the burden of stop loss is not extraordinarily harsh on those soldiers forced to continue fighting in Iraq and Afghanistan long after their enlistment agreements have expired. Considering the sacrifice and service to the country required of all soldiers, nonconsensual extensions are particularly distasteful and unfair if the military makes no effort to actually inform the soldiers of that possibility upon enlistment. Furthermore, there is strong evidence that cutbacks in troop levels by Congress and the past two presidents were excessive and are in part responsible for the conditions leading to stop loss. Nonetheless, as discussed above, it was also Congress's intent to give the President the power to exercise stop loss authority in undeclared wars such as in Iraq and Afghanistan. And past decisions show that courts view enlistment agreements as quite distinct from private and civilian contracts, stemming from both the unique status of soldiers as well as the paramount need of the state to exercise war powers in order to preserve itself. Courts are therefore likely to be highly deferential to Congress's decision to grant the President stop loss authority.

In deciding the lawsuits challenging extensions in Iraq under stop loss, courts will of course have to consider the precedent they would create for nonconsensual extensions in future conflicts. Arguments that stop loss is fundamentally "shameful" and "a breach of trust" would likely resonate much less if not for the increasingly accepted view that the Iraqi conflict was not in fact necessary to protect U.S. national security. It is not difficult to imagine scenarios—such as if terrorists again conducted a major attack on the United States with the benefit of safe harbor given by foreign governments—in which such nonconsensual extensions might truly be necessary to protect the security of the United States, even where Congress would never formally declare war. For public policy considerations, in addition to strict construction of the statutes and reasons of stare decisis, courts are unlikely to rule that the President may not exercise stop loss powers, even if doing so breaches soldiers' enlistment agreements.

However, considering the substantial sacrifice made by all enlistees, the military should at the very least take steps to ensure enlistees are aware of the various scenarios under which their service may be extended without their consent. The most straightforward way of doing so might be to revise its standard Enlistment/Reenlistment Document in order to advise enlistees of the possibility of nonconsensual extension. It could do so by simply adding the following subparagraph under Paragraph 10:

> FOR ALL ENLISTEES: Whenever any member of a reserve component has been ordered to active duty in a time of national emergency declared by the President of the United States, or in time of war or national emergency declared by the Congress, or when the President has determined that such activation is necessary to support any operational mission, my military service may be extended without my consent for as long as any such reservist remains on active duty.

The difficult issues raised by stop loss ultimately have their source in the state's power to compel citizens to fight in military combat, even if doing so causes them to risk serious injury or death. Nonconsensual military service in one form or another appears to be inevitable so long as the United States decides to engage in military confrontations beyond the capacity of the permanent all volunteer force. However, if the government is going to use stop loss to conscript those who volunteered to serve in the first place, it at least owes new enlistees a complete disclosure of all the scenarios in which their enlistment might be extended without their consent.

Periodical Bibliography

The following articles have been selected to supplement the diverse views presented in this chapter.

Jonathan Alter	"We're Dodging the Draft Issue," *Newsweek*, October 4, 2004.
Andrew J. Bacevich	"Who's Bearing the Burden? Iraq and the Demise of the All-Volunteer Army," *Commonweal*, July 15, 2005.
Sandra I. Erwin	"Obliged to Add Troops, the Army Agonizes over Costs," *National Defense*, December 2004.
Heidi Golding et al.	"The All-Volunteer Military: Issues and Performance," *Congressional Budget Office*, July 2007.
William Norman Grigg	"Get Ready for the Draft," *New American*, May 30, 2005.
Winston Groom	"An Army of 50 Million? The Surprisingly Dishonest Draft Debate," *Weekly Standard*, December 11, 2006.
Tim Kane	"CBO Weighs In on the All-Volunteer Force," *Heritage Foundation Web Memo no. 1561*, July 20, 2007.
Fred Kaplan	"Draft Numbers," *Slate*, August 14, 2007.
Bill Maxwell	"Time to Bring Back the Military Draft," *St. Petersburg Times*, November 5, 2006.
Patricia Smith	"Is It Time to Bring Back the Draft?" *New York Times Upfront*, January 15, 2007.
W. Thomas Smith Jr.	"One Democrat's Deception," *National Review*, November 29, 2006.
Jacob Weisberg	"Rough Draft," *Slate*, March 22, 2006.
Wilson Quarterly	"A Return to the Draft?" vol. 29, no. 4, Autumn 2005.

CHAPTER 2

How Would the Draft Affect U.S. Society?

Chapter Preface

The antiwar, antidraft movement that bitterly divided the U.S. public during the Vietnam War subsided with the abolition of the draft in 1973 and withdrawal of U.S. troops from Vietnam in 1975. As antiwar activist Edward Hasbrouck wrote in 2005, "Since the 1980s, there's been no national single-issue antidraft organization in the United States. The only national groups focused primarily on the draft are devoted to the rights of conscientious objectors within the system and don't advocate resistance."

But Hasbrouck's 2005 prediction that, organized or not, people would soon be talking about the draft, and draft resistance, again in large numbers has come true. Despite Pentagon assurances that military planners are not considering the reinstatement of the military draft and that the all-volunteer army is effectively meeting U.S. defense needs, the protracted war in Iraq and concerns about overstretched volunteer forces have sparked widely dispersed antiwar, antidraft sentiment that cannot yet be considered a movement but nonetheless exposes in 2007 rifts in American society.

Tens of thousands of people staged an antiwar demonstration on the National Mall in Washington, D.C., in January 2007 and a march on the Pentagon (and other major cities) two months later. Antiwar, anti-recruitiing rallies drew hundreds in New York City and thousands in Kennebunkport, Maine, in August 2007. Grass-roots groups—Mothers Against the Draft, Veterans for Peace, the Granny Peace Brigade— emerged alongside established organizations such as the San Diego-based Committee Opposed to Militarism and the Draft and the War Resisters League in New York City.

But as in the 1960s, demonstrations have been accompanied by angry clashes between war protesters and war supporters. Participants in the March 2007 march on the Pentagon, for example, were flanked by lines of thousands of veterans and others who waved signs supporting the Bush administration's Iraq policy and fell into shouting matches with marchers.

James Jay Carafano, a senior research fellow for defense and homeland security at the conservative think tank Heritage Foundation in Washington, D.C., wrote in 2004, "A draft today . . . likely would be as socially divisive as Vietnam-era conscription." But advocates of the return to the draft such as Representative Charles Rangel argue that Vietnam-era opposition to the draft was rooted in its discriminatory application; the burden of service fell disproportionately on the working class and the poor, inequities Rangel says a present-day draft could be designed to avoid. The authors of the viewpoints in the following chapter debate the effects of conscription on a new generation of Americans fighting an increasingly unpopular war.

> "[Mandatory national service] would ... rekindle a sense of shared national purpose. And it isn't right or left, Democratic or Republican."

A Draft Would Unify U.S. Society

Hodding Carter and Ronald Goldfarb

Hodding Carter, University Professor of Leadership and Public Policy at the University of North Carolina at Chapel Hill, served in the U.S. Marine Corps and as former assistant secretary of state under President Jimmy Carter. Washington, D.C., attorney and author Ronald Goldfarb served in the air force and investigated organized crime and racketeering in the Justice Department under President John F. Kennedy. In the following viewpoint, Carter and Goldfarb point to their military and public service with pride and argue that mandatory national service would give young Americans what it gave them: uncynical patriotism and a shared sense of national purpose, understanding and appreciation of diversity, and personal maturity.

As you read, consider the following questions:

1. How do the authors answer the question, What does the citizen owe the state?
2. How long a term of mandatory service do Carter and Goldfarb advocate?
3. What kinds of service would fulfill a person's obligation, according to the authors?

As with so many Americans of our generation, we went into military service because that was what you were expected to do. We may have groused at the time, but we are proud of having served our country. It carved a few years out of our lives in the 1950s and '60s, but strengthened our understanding of the country we served and the people with whom we served.

Of course, while public service now seems self-evident to us, it does not to most of our children's generation. It is not that they turn away from duty to the civil society. Millions have chosen the military, of course. Many serve in the government and voluntary service organizations, working among the urban poor and rural landless. A large number tell pollsters they believe in volunteerism. But the idea of public service as a universal duty is another story.

On the campaign trail these days [late 2006], there are few fresh ideas, and in the wake of the fifth 9/11 anniversary, there are still not enough calls for public sacrifice beyond that made by our troops. National service isn't a new idea. It arises from one of the oldest themes of U.S. history. What does the citizen owe the state? Answer: mandated public service without exemptions.

Tapping Patriotism

Mandatory national service could appeal to Americans' natural inclination toward patriotism and provide an antidote to the cynical public attitude that characterizes recent politics. It

The Benefits of Conscription

The United States benefits from conscription because national spirit increases, national unity improves, neighborhoods become safer, and society grows healthier. With conscription, troubled teens who normally head to street corners enter the military and receive the training, discipline and experience that propel them to a stable and secure life. They unite with people of all sexes, races and religions to work toward a common good. This allows neighborhoods to become safer and society to become stronger. The workforce gets better workers, families get better mothers and fathers, and the country gets a more unified citizenship.

Armstrong Williams,
"Mandatory Military Service Would Benefit the U.S.,"
NewsMax.com, *June 19, 2006,*
http://archive.newsmax.com/archives/articles/2006/6/18/162837.shtml.

would bring out the best in young Americans and rekindle a sense of shared national purpose. And it isn't right or left, Democratic or Republican.

The death of the military draft was hailed in the Vietnam War era by liberals and conservatives alike, not necessarily for shared reasons but with shared acclaim. With today's professionalized military, the many are protected; the relative few fight and die in the name of the whole.

The best approach to mandatory national service would be to require every 18-year-old man and woman, and every young immigrant seeking citizenship, to spend 18 months to two years in public service. Their service could be in the military or in the Homeland Security Department, or be in programs similar to President Franklin Roosevelt's Civilian Conservation Corps, Sargent Shriver's Peace Corps or President Clinton's AmeriCorps—any work experience that is in the public interest.

The First Class

According to the Bureau of Labor Statistics, there are about 4 million 18-year-olds who might fill our proposed first class. Some 2.7 million youths graduated from high school from 2004 through 2005. Just under 60,000 are in the military. Others hold jobs, are in school or are in jail. About 17% are unemployed.

There are great costs attributable to this class, economic and others. The cost of public service would be a wise investment. After completing national service, these young people would enter their next phase in life more mature and more knowledgeable about the rich variety of America's peoples and the breadth of the nation's unfinished business.

National service is not a partisan concept. Sen. John McCain, R-Ariz., has praised Clinton's AmeriCorps program. It also need not be the exclusive province of government. Private-public interest organizations, including churches and other faith-based groups, could qualify as sponsors and providers of public service. Diversity, rather than bureaucratic uniformity, would be encouraged.

But the bottom line would be the reinstitution of a notion as old as the nation. Just as all share in the benefits of freedom, all should share in shoring it up.

"The draft's perennial unpopularity stems from an abiding national regard for freedom from state coercion."

A Draft Would Divide U.S. Society

David Greenberg

Look back in U.S. history, David Greenberg argues in the following viewpoint, and see that the military draft has always been divisive and not, as draft supporters claim, a unifying experience. The concept of conscripted citizen-soldiers bonding in shared sacrifice, as well as appeals to patriotism and democracy, has been part of political rhetoric for hundreds of years, but it is an illusion, Greenberg maintains: Americans value equality but they value personal liberty more, and they abhor state coercion. The Minute Men of the Revolutionary War were volunteers, draftees in the American Revolution and Civil War paid mostly poor people to take their place, and the unpopularity of World War I and the Vietnam War led to bitter protest over the draft in their eras, he points out, and there is no reason to think a new draft would be any more palatable or equitable. David Greenberg is a professor of history and media studies at Rutgers University and the author of a biography of Calvin Coolidge.

As you read, consider the following questions:

1. How does the wording of the Constitution reflect its drafters' opposition to military conscription, according to the author?

2. What kinds of social protest did the World War I–era draft provoke, according to Greenberg?

3. On what point does the author agree with Rep. Charles Rangel, who advocates reinstituting the draft?

The draft is back—or at least back on the table. Rep. Charles Rangel, D-N.Y., is fronting a group of anti-war leftists sounding a theme more commonly heard in conservative and neoliberal circles: that in our anomic culture we need mandatory service to instill common values, provide a shared experience for young people of all races and social stripes, and equitably spread the burden of military service. Writing in the *New York Times*, Rangel urged a "return to the tradition of the citizen soldier," arguing that "if we are going to send our children to war, the governing principle must be that of shared sacrifice."

State Coercion Has Always Been a Tough Sell

Cries like Rangel's have arisen in every war and quite often in peace as well. In 1940, inaugurating the first-ever peacetime draft, Franklin Roosevelt argued that the new policy "broadened and enriched our basic concepts of citizenship." A quarter century later, Lyndon Johnson called the draft "a part of America, a part of the process of our democracy." Indeed, appeals to patriotism and democracy have often accompanied the imposition of mandatory sacrifice.

Despite these fine words, though, conscription has always been—and probably will always be—a tough sell. The reason isn't that Americans crave an unjust system, although they haven't shown too much regret over the draft's inequities. Rather, the draft's perennial unpopularity stems from an abiding national regard for freedom from state coercion. For all Rangel's rhetorical bows to the "citizen soldier" and "shared sacrifice," his proposal addresses America's historic concern for equality but skirts its even more primary veneration for liberty.

Indeed, the notion of the citizen soldier of the Revolutionary War to which Rangel hearkens—the common man trading plowshare for sword to fight an imminent threat—actually points up the flaws in the argument for conscription. The Revolution's vaunted Minute Men were, after all, volunteers who needed no official prodding to take up arms against a threat to their liberty. The Continental Army certainly had its manpower problems—in the winter of 1776, Tom Paine decried the "summer soldier and the sunshine patriot"—but even in those trying times, states rejected George Washington's plea for national conscription. When individual states did hold drafts, they allowed wealthy conscripts to hire substitutes, who were predominantly poor and unemployed. Service was hardly a shared experience.

Whatever problems hobbled the Continental Army, the new nation's founders remained convinced that state encroachment on personal freedom was the greater danger. The Constitution's drafters conferred on Congress the power to "raise and support armies" but not to conscript citizens—an omission notably at odds with the practice in Europe. Virginia's Edmund Randolph, one of the few founders to raise the issue during the constitutional debates, argued that a draft would "stretch the strings of government too violently to be adopted." Such sentiments carried the day even when British troops invaded American soil two decades later. During the War of 1812, President James Madison sought a draft. But even though Secretary of War James Monroe promised it would be just a temporary, emergency measure, Congress op-

Americans Would Fight Conscription

A draft [would be] more divisive and disastrous than ever before in the nation's history, exposing deep fissures in the civic psyche. . . .

What you have is a growing class of Americans who would fight conscription with neither reservation nor remorse. This includes not simply the functional equivalent of the 19-year-olds burning their draft cards a generation ago, but the parents of many of today's 19-year-olds as well. The divisions over the war in Iraq and growing mistrust about the justification for the invasion have resulted in a middle-aged middle class who have adapted the old slogan to cover their own kids: hell no, they won't go.

Anna Quindlen, "Leaving on a Jet Plane," Newsweek, September 6, 2004, www.msnbc.msn.com/id/5852831/site/newsweek.

posed it, in Sen. Daniel Webster's words, as "Napoleonic despotism." It never got off the ground.

Conscription Divided the Nation in the Civil War and WW I

In the Civil War, both North and South continued to rely mainly on enlistment, although they did adopt conscription when the volunteers dried up. Even though the Civil War drafts were extremely limited—only 8 percent of [the] Union's 2 million soldiers were draftees—they were far from successful. The Confederate government gave exemptions to those in certain occupations, sparking popular protest. Meanwhile, the delegation of such vast powers to the Confederate government baldly violated the principle of "states' rights" and undermined the South's rationale for its rebellion.

The North had similar headaches. Its practice of letting draftees buy their way out of service for $300—a laborer's yearly income—led critics to dub the conflict "a rich man's war but a poor man's fight." In New York, enforcement efforts, as anyone who's seen *Gangs of New York* will know, triggered ferocious riots that killed more than 100 people,including many young blacks who the conscripted Irish workers lynched as scapegoats.

Fifty years later, with Europe at war, Woodrow Wilson courted the animosity of isolationists left and right by pushing through Congress a sweeping (but temporary) conscription program. To ensure fairness, the law barred the hiring of substitutes and the offering of bounties for enlistees. But the draft's more fundamental flaw—its coerciveness—still fueled protest. Waves of conscripts, perhaps as many as 3 million, refused to register for the draft, and of those actually called to serve, 12 percent either didn't report or quickly deserted. Local vigilantes took to shaming or brutalizing resisters into service. Civil libertarians sued the government, arguing that the draft was unconstitutional under the 13th Amendment, which outlawed involuntary servitude, but in 1918 the Supreme Court upheld it as constitutional.

The draft was scuttled when peace returned, but in 1940, when Germany invaded France, FDR sought to resurrect it. Again, opposition was fierce; Sen. Arthur Vandenberg, for one, accused FDR of "tearing up 150 years of American history and tradition, in which none but volunteers have entered the peacetime Armies and Navies." But FDR won out, and resistance faded after Pearl Harbor. As it was in so many ways, the experience of the "good" war proved an exception to a historical pattern. Yet FDR's policies also set a precedent for the more questionable Cold War draft, which would last 25 years.

In March 1947, President Truman spoke of his "earnest desire of placing our Army and Navy on an entirely volunteer basis" as soon as possible—a desire that was clearly shared by a public eager to return to normalcy. But one year later, he reversed course, calling for universal service, and a House committee endorsed the proposal, citing the "serious deterioration in the international situation." Critics limited the peacetime draft to a two-year trial run, after which it would have to be renewed. But Cold War battle lines were hardening, and at each expiration date over the next decade, congressional opposition diminished.

Charles Rangel Was Wrong in 1971 and He's Wrong Now

It took the catastrophe of Vietnam to end the draft. By the late 1960s, the mounting body counts and anti-war sentiment made it increasingly hard for President Johnson to justify sending young men to die in battle. Until 1969, Maj. Gen. Lewis B. Hershey, the head of the Selective Service, blocked efforts to reform or end the draft, but when Richard Nixon assumed the presidency he saw draft reform as a way to silence the peace movement and steal the Democrats' thunder without a precipitous pullout. Nixon forced Hershey into retirement, set up a lottery to make the draft fairer, and indicated he would move toward an all-volunteer force (AVF). In a debate over whether to continue the draft in 1971 or adopt an AVF, it was Nixon and Gen. William Westmoreland who argued for the AVF, while leading Democrats in Congress such as Ted Kennedy and one Charlie Rangel pressed to keep the draft in place.

In an April 17, 1971, piece in the *New York Times*, Rangel argued that the proposed "volunteer" force would be "a lie." Poor minorities, in need of employment, would wind up volunteering and "doing the white man's dirty work," he wrote, while "white Americans could then sip cocktails and watch the black Hessians make war on their color television sets, just like the plantation owners who sipped mint juleps on their verandas and watched the darkies toiling in the fields." Rangel insisted then—as he insists about his calls for conscription today—that he wasn't being facetious to prove a point, that he believes a draft would be better than our current military.

But Rangel also wrote in his 1971 article, "There is only one way this country can get its young to loyally perform military service. It must begin to institute morally just foreign . . . policies." He may have been overstating the case; whether or not young people will gladly head into battle probably doesn't hinge on the justness of the war. But with this much Charlie Rangel surely still agrees: Without a just war, it's impossible to have a just draft.

> *"Since the late 1990s, the military—particularly the Army—has been having trouble meeting its recruiting goals, leading to a decline in the quality of recruits."*

A Draft Would Improve Declining Troop Quality

Michelle Cottle

The military is suffering acute personnel shortages, thanks largely to the protracted war in Iraq, and has been forced to lower its recruiting standards to fill the ranks, writes Michelle Cottle in the following viewpoint. According to Cottle, the army has been forced to accept many more volunteers who lack a high school diploma, raise incentive bonuses that amount to creating a mercenary force of cash-strapped enlistees with few other options in life, and even resort to "desperate tactics" that include coaching a prospective enlistee on how to cheat on a drug test and signing up a volunteer with a documented history of mental illness. Mandatory service, including military conscription, must be considered to maintain national security with a high-tech military increasingly dependent on bright, well-trained personnel, she

Michelle Cottle, "Draft Pick," *New Republic*, June 17, 2005. Copyright © 2005 by The New Republic, Inc. Reproduced by permission of The *New Republic*.

concludes. Michelle Cottle is a senior editor at The New Republic, *a bimonthly political opinion magazine known for its support of progressive and liberal policy.*

As you read, consider the following questions:

1. How much has the percentage of troops deemed
   "high quality" dropped in the all-volunteer army
   between 1992 and 1999, according to Cottle?
2. What percentage of 2005 enlistees lacks a high
   school diploma, and what percentage score in the
   lowest acceptable category on army aptitude tests,
   according to the author?
3. By how much is the army missing its recruitment
   targets, according to figures quoted by Cottle?

I've never been comfortable with the idea of a military
draft—considerably less so since I became a mom. . . .

But opposing a draft on purely selfish grounds doesn't exactly make one glow with pride or patriotism. As such, I've always taken great comfort in the fact that military professionals
are generally opposed to conscription, too, but for pragmatic,
performance-based reasons. These are, after all, the people
presumably in the best position to know what serves the needs
of our armed forces. Among the most compelling and commonly cited of their objections are the deep personal commitment and higher quality of recruits provided by an all-
volunteer force—with the latter advantage becoming ever
more vital as our military becomes ever more reliant on high-
tech weapons systems that require bright, well-trained personnel to operate.

High-Quality Enlistees Dropped
from 74 to 59 Percent

Unfortunately, since the late 1990s, the military—particularly
the Army—has been having trouble meeting its recruiting
goals, leading to a decline in the quality of recruits. As noted

by the *Washington Monthly* (for which resurrecting the draft has long been a pet cause) between 1992 and 1999 the percentage of enlistees deemed "high quality" dropped from 74 percent to 59 percent. Thanks to the nightmare in Iraq, that situation has grown dramatically worse in recent months [as of June 2005]. As revealed both by independent media reports and the military's own recruiting data, the Army in particular is being forced to use some pretty desperate tactics to come anywhere close to meeting its (already scaled back) recruiting targets. In the process, the service is undercutting many of the arguments against a draft and highlighting some of the most troubling features of our all-volunteer force.

First and most importantly, the quality of our troops is in jeopardy. The news of late has been filled with accounts of how stressed-out Army recruiters have been breaking all the rules in order to meet their monthly quotas. Reported violations have included Colorado recruiters coaching a prospective enlistee on how to fake a high school diploma and cheat on his drug test; a Houston recruiter threatening to have a prospect arrested if he didn't show up at the recruiting station; and an Ohio recruiter signing up a young man with a documented history of mental illness. According to the *New York Times*, the Army's own stats show that substantiated cases of recruiting improprieties rose more than 60 percent between 1999 and 2004. Confronted with this new round of abuse charges, the service actually suspended recruitment for a day in order to reinstruct its personnel on the ethical dos and don'ts of enlistment.

More Recruits Lack a High School Diploma

Just as troubling as the anecdotal evidence of misconduct by recruiters is the general lowering of standards. [In 2005] the number of Army enlistees without a high school diploma rose from 8 to 10 percent, the maximum level allowed. Similarly, the number of enlistees scoring in the lowest acceptable cat-

Recruits with Criminal Backgrounds and Medical Problems

The number of waivers granted to Army recruits with criminal backgrounds has grown about 65 percent in the last three years, increasing to 8,129 in 2006 from 4,918 in 2003, Department of Defense records show. . . .

It has also increased the number of so-called "moral waivers" to recruits with criminal pasts, even as the total number of recruits dropped slightly. The sharpest increase was in waivers for serious misdemeanors, which make up the bulk of all the Army's moral waivers. These include aggravated assault, burglary, robbery and vehicular homicide. . . .

The Defense Department has also expanded its applicant pool by accepting soldiers with . . . medical problems like asthma, high blood pressure and attention deficit disorder, situations that require waivers. Medical waivers have increased 4 percent, totaling 12,313 in 2006. Without waivers, the soldiers would have been barred from service.

Lizette Alvarez, "Army Giving More Waivers in Recruiting,"
The New York Times, February 14, 2007.

egory on the military's vocational aptitude test also has risen to meet the Army's upper limit of 2 percent of recruits.

But the Army has been compelled to do more than just stretch its quality standards to the limit. Now, rather than a 2-year minimum enlistment, recruits are being offered a shortened stint of only 15 months. This abbreviated enlistment, experts warn, means an abbreviated training period and less-prepared troops being shipped off to combat. Of course, these days the Army is increasingly employing its "stop loss" program, which involuntarily keeps soldiers on active duty beyond their agreed-upon enlistment period. So it's entirely possible that these less well-trained soldiers will wind up spending a full two years in the service anyway, regardless of what their recruiters promised them.

These sorts of shenanigans do not seem to be helping. May 2005 was the fourth consecutive month in which the Army missed its recruitment target (by a full 25 percent this time), even after having lowered its monthly goal from 8,050 to 6,700. The Army National Guard and Reserve are having similar problems despite upping the eligible enrollment age from 35 to 39.

Incentive Bonuses Are Creating a Lower-Quality Mercenary Force

Its back against the wall, the Army has resorted to that most reliable of incentives: money. The service doubled its signing bonus to $40,000. From a certain perspective, this could be cheered as recognition of the invaluable service our recruits are providing their country. The less rosy view is that the Army is dangling increasingly irresistible bribes in front of cash-strapped young people—intensifying the existing inequity of a military where the non-wealthy do the dangerous job of safeguarding the freedoms of the more privileged, who in turn have the luxury of not volunteering to get their asses blown up. The creation of a mercenary fighting force, many of whose members signed on because they had few other life options, cannot be what military professionals have in mind when they sing the praises of an all-volunteer corps.

With the military's operational objections to the draft being eroded by its own policies, all those soaring, idealistic arguments in favor of national service start to gain ground: the fundamental justness of expecting all Americans to share in the greatest of citizenship burdens; the need to foster a shared sense of national purpose among young people from all walks of life; the need for the nation's elites to better understand the military, if only to make well-informed decisions about its structure and function. And when you check out the sorts of draft proposals that have been floated in recent years—which include assigning most conscripts (as opposed to volunteer recruits) to support jobs rather than combat posts or combining the draft with a mandatory national service program that makes military service just one of several options—the idea starts to look frighteningly sensible.

Indeed, if the military's manpower crisis continues apace, and the lower quality and quantity of recruits starts to undermine our national security, basically the only argument that will soon be left against the draft is that it is politically infeasible. But this would require effectively admitting that we are determined to let an unrepresentative slice of America shoulder our defense burden (and inadequately at that) just to avoid pissing off affluent, politically potent soccer moms—like me. I'm not sure how long even our utterly politically self-serving congressmen could compromise our collective security on such shaky grounds—especially with no end in sight to the war in Iraq, much less the broader war on terror. And my own maternal fears notwithstanding, I'm not sure how long I would want them to.

"In many criteria, each year shows advancement, not decline, in measureable qualities of new enlistees."

There Is No Evidence That Troop Quality Has Declined in the All-Volunteer Army

Tim Kane

The accusation that the all-volunteer military is "accepting unqualified enlistees in a futile attempt to meet its recruiting goals in the midst of an unpopular war" is demonstrably untrue, economic policy expert Tim Kane argues in the following viewpoint. Kane presents a range of Department of Defense and Census Bureau data for enlistees in all branches from 2003 to 2005 to show that recruits have far higher high school graduation rates than youths nationwide, continue to pursue college and advanced degrees in the course of military service, and have higher reading levels than the youth population in general. Furthermore, he maintains, the percentage of "high quality" recruits as determined by military aptitude tests has increased, not decreased, between 2001 and 2005. Kane concludes that recruit quality remains high, recruiting standards do not need alter-

Tim Kane, *Heritage Foundation Report CDA06-09*. Washington, DC: Heritage Foundation, 2006. Copyright © 2006 The Heritage Foundation. Reproduced by permission.

ation, and the draft does not need to be reinstated. Tim Kane is director of the Center for International Trade and Economics at the conservative think tank the Heritage Foundation in Washington, D.C., and lead author of the foundation's annual Index of Economic Freedom.

As you read, consider the following questions:

1. What is the only demographic group that has lowered its participation in the military between 1999 and 2005, according to Kane?

2. As reported by Kane, what percentage of active-duty officers held bachelor's degrees or higher in 2004?

3. What was the percentage of high quality recruits in 2001 and in 2005, according to the author?

A pillar of conventional wisdom about the U.S. military is that the quality of volunteers has been degraded after the invasions of Afghanistan and Iraq. Examples of the voices making this claim range from the *Washington Post, Los Angeles Times,* and New York *Daily News* to Michael Moore's pseudo-documentary *Fahrenheit 9/11*. Some insist that minorities and the underprivileged are overrepresented in the military. Others accuse the U.S. Army of accepting unqualified enlistees in a futile attempt to meet its recruiting goals in the midst of an unpopular war.

A report published by The Heritage Foundation in November 2005 examined the issue and could not substantiate any degradation in troop quality by comparing military enlistees in 1999 to those in 2003. It is possible that troop quality did not degrade until after the initial invasion of Iraq in 2003, when patriotism was high. A common assumption is that the Army experienced difficulty getting qualified enlistees in 2005 and was subsequently forced to lower its standards. This report revisits the issue by examining the full recruiting classes for all branches of the U.S. military for every year from 2003 to 2005.

Troop Quality Is Rising, Not Declining

The current findings show that the demographic characteristics of volunteers have continued to show signs of higher, not lower, quality. Quality is a difficult concept to apply to soldiers, or to human beings in any context, and it should be understood here in context. Regardless of the standards used to screen applicants, the average quality of the people accepted into any organization can be assessed only by using measurable criteria, which surely fail to account for intangible characteristics. In the military, it is especially questionable to claim that measurable characteristics accurately reflect what really matters: courage, honor, integrity, loyalty, and leadership.

Those who have been so quick to suggest that today's wartime recruits represent lesser quality, lower standards, or lower class should be expected make an airtight case. Instead, they have cited selective evidence, which is balanced by a much clearer set of evidence showing improving troop quality.

Indeed, in many criteria, each year shows advancement, not decline, in measurable qualities of new enlistees. For example, it is commonly claimed that the military relies on recruits from poorer neighborhoods because the wealthy will not risk death in war. This claim has been advanced without any rigorous evidence. Our review of Pentagon enlistee data shows that the only group that is lowering its participation in the military is the poor. The percentage of recruits from the poorest American neighborhoods (with one-fifth of the U.S. population) declined from 18 percent in 1999 to 14.6 percent in 2003, 14.1 percent in 2004, and 13.7 percent in 2005.

This report updates the previous Heritage Foundation report, with data on all U.S. recruits during 2004 and 2005. We introduce the term "wartime recruits" to identify volunteer enlistees in all branches during 2003, 2004, and 2005. Like the previous report, the analysis considers the following characteristics:

- Household income,

- Level of education,

- Race/ethnicity, and

- Regional/rural origin.

Demographic Evidence Shatters Pro-Draft Arguments

In summary, the additional years of recruit data (2004–2005) support the previous finding that U.S. military recruits are more similar than dissimilar to the American youth population. The slight differences are that wartime U.S. military enlistees are better educated, wealthier, and more rural on average than their civilian peers.

Recruits have a higher percentage of high school graduates and representation from southern and rural areas. No evidence indicates exploitation of racial minorities (either by race or by race-weighted ZIP code areas). Finally, the distribution of household income of recruits is noticeably higher than that of the entire youth population.

Demographic evidence discredits the argument that a draft is necessary to enforce representation from racial and socioeconomic groups. Additionally, three of the four branches of the armed forces met their recruiting goals in fiscal year 2005, and Army reenlistments are the highest in the past five years. A draft is not necessary to increase the size of the active-duty forces. Our analysis using Pentagon data on wartime volunteers effectively shatters the case for reinstating the draft. . . .

Education

Educational achievement is the characteristic most commonly cited as evidence of lower military standards driven by the

Military Standards Would Be Watered Down for an Army of Draftees

Today's recruits come primarily from the middle class, and, more importantly, they come willingly. This makes them more amenable to training and more likely to adapt to the rigors of military culture. An Army of draftees would so expand the number of recruits that training resources would inevitably be stretched and standards watered down. Meanwhile, scarce resources would be devoted to tens of thousands of temporary soldiers who planned to leave as soon as their year or two of forced service was up.

Wall Street Journal, *"Uncle Charlie Wants You!"*
Opinion Journal, *November 25, 2006,*
www.opinionjournal.com/weekend/hottopic/?id=110009302.

Iraq War. While some measures, such as the higher percentage of Category IV recruits [who score in the lowest third on armed forces aptitude tests, between 10 and 30 points out of 100] in the Army, are cited, other measures, such as the higher percentage of Category I [scores between 93 and 100] recruits, are ignored. In general, the higher quality of recruits compared to equivalent civilian population has held steady during the war years.

The previous study noted the significant difference between the national recruit high school graduation rate of 98 percent and the national youth graduation rate of 75 percent. This strong distinction continues among the 2004 and 2005 recruits when compared to the national educational attainment levels reported by the Census 2004 American Community Survey (ACS).

Given the nature of the military rank structure, most enlisted recruits do not have a college education or degree. Members of the armed forces with higher education are more often commissioned officers (lieutenant and above). In 2004, 92.1 percent of active-duty officer accessions held baccalaureate degrees or higher. From 2000 to 2005, between 10 percent and 17 percent of active-duty officer accessions held advanced degrees, and between 35 percent and 45 percent of the active-duty officer corps held advanced degrees. This indicates that officers continued their education during the course of their military service.

Many enlisted personnel are drawn to the benefits offered by the armed forces that allow them to obtain funding for college. In recent years, incentives to join the military have increased, providing more of the enlisted recruits with additional resources to finance their education. Although only about 7 percent of recruits for 2003–2005 entered the military with some college experience, over 11 percent of the 2004 active component enlisted force had some college experience.

Additionally, in the most recent edition of *Population Representation in the Military Services*, the Department of Defense reported that the mean reading level of 2004 recruits is a full grade level higher than that of the comparable youth population. Fewer than 2 percent of wartime recruits have no high school credentials. . . . The national high school graduation rate taken from the Census 2004 ACS is 79.8 percent. . . .

The military defines a "high quality" recruit as one who has scored above the 50th percentile on the AFQT and has a high school diploma. The percentage of high-quality recruits has increased from 57 percent in 2001 to 64 percent in 2005 (67 percent in 2004), indicating not only that the military is accepting intelligent and well-educated recruits, but also that the representation of these recruits has increased strongly since the 9/11 terrorist attacks.

While the military has changed its policies to allow flexibility in recruiting standards, it has certainly not abandoned them. The current guidelines allow each force the flexibility to accept recruits who satisfy only one criterion: either a high school diploma or an above-average score on the AFQT, which is a standard equal to or exceeding the general youth population. . . .

Military Ranks Represent the Nation

As support for the war in Iraq has declined, criticism of the war has translated into criticism of our nation's troops, at least by way of criticizing the quality of wartime recruits. The November 2005 Heritage Foundation study found that recruits enlisting at the start of the war were of high quality and in many respects comparable to the youth population. This updated report's examination of three years of wartime recruits shows that recruit quality has not declined.

The estimate for mean household income of recruits increased every year from 2003 through 2005. The poorest areas continue to be underrepresented, while middle-class areas are overrepresented. Although the richest income brackets are underrepresented, the difference between the recruit and population proportions for these brackets is less than 0.25 percent. Overall, the distribution for recruit household incomes is very similar to that of the youth population.

The military continues to enforce educational standards in its recruiting process. The high school graduation rate among recruits is higher than it is among the national youth population. While the active-duty enlisted ranks have fewer college graduates than the comparable civilian population, DOD annual updates on population representation indicate that many who join the military are taking advantage of educational opportunities while serving and that many others continue their education after completing their enlistment period.

The enlisted ranks are not disproportionately composed of minorities. Whites serve in numbers roughly proportional to their representation in the population. While blacks continue to be overrepresented, their representation has decreased during the wartime years and is much closer to being proportional in 2005 than it was in 2003. Additionally, recruiters are not targeting black-concentrated areas in an effort to exploit the black population.

Wartime recruits come more from rural areas, particularly from the South. However, many states outside of the South, such as Alaska and Montana, continue to have strong proportional representation. Areas classified as entirely urban are strongly underrepresented compared to areas with increased rural concentrations, all of which were overrepresented.

Overall, the wartime recruits are more similar than dissimilar to their civilian counterparts. The all-volunteer force displays near proportional representation of income backgrounds. Whites serve in approximate proportion to their population, although representation of minority groups varies. Recruits must meet educational standards, and the military provides resources for furthering education to those who might not otherwise have the opportunity to attend four-year colleges. Although rural representation is disproportional, the military offers the opportunity to gain new skills and enter industries that are not available in rural areas.

With regard to income, education, race, and regional background, the all-volunteer force is representative of our nation and meets standards set by Congress and the Department of Defense. In contrast to the patronizing slanders of antiwar critics, recruit quality is increasing as the war in Iraq continues. Although recent recruiting goals have been difficult to meet, reenlistment is strong and recruit quality remains high. No evidence supports arguments for reinstating the draft or altering recruiting policies to achieve more equitable representation.

Periodical Bibliography

The following articles have been selected to supplement the diverse views presented in this chapter.

Frida Berrigan   "Oh Baby, It's Drafty Out There," *AlterNet.org*, July 5, 2005, www.alternet.org/story/23308.

Drew Brown   "Supporters Say Draft Would Spread War Burden: Privileged Youth Aren't Doing Their Part," *Columbus (GA) Ledger-Enquirer*, January 29, 2007.

Tim Cavanaugh   "Middle-Class Warfare: Military Recruits and Poverty," *Reason*, March 2006.

Katarina Keller, Panu Poutvaara, and Andreas Wagener   "Military Draft and Economic Growth in OECD [Organization for Economic Cooperation and Development] Countries," IZA Discussion Paper No. 2022, *Institute for the Study of Labor*, March 2006, http://ftp.iza.org/dp2022.pdf.

Hisam Kim   "The Military Draft and Career Disruption," Job Market Paper, Department of Economics, University of Wisconsin-Madison, November 24, 2005, www.ssc.wisc.edu/˜hikim/Draftee_penalty.pdf.

Jorge Mariscal   "The Poverty Draft: Do Military Recruiters Disproportionately Target Communities of Color and the Poor?" *Sojourner*, June 2007.

Pamela M. Prah   "Draft Debates: Draft Resistance," *CQ Researcher*, August 19, 2005.

Thomas Sowell   "A Military Draft?" *Townhall.com*, August 1, 2006.

Joan Vennochi   "A Military Draft Might Awaken Us," *Boston Globe*, June 22, 2006.

Jacob Weisberg   "Rough Draft: The Gross Unfairness of an All-Volunteer Army," *Slate*, March 22, 2006.

OPPOSING
VIEWPOINTS®
SERIES

CHAPTER 3

Who Should Be Subject to a Military Draft?

Chapter Preface

The last time Americans were subject to a military draft was during the Vietnam War era, 1964–1973, when more than 1.8 million men were inducted into the armed forces through the Selective Service System (SSS). "Greetings" the SSS draft notice read: "Having submitted yourself to a Local Board composed of your neighbors for the purpose of determining your availability for service in the Armed Forces of the United States, you are hereby ordered to report." Then as now, the SSS was responsible for providing soldiers to the military when they were needed; then as now, there was heated debate over who should be required to serve and who should not.

Millions of Americans of draft age in the Vietnam era never received a draft notice because they were women and thereby ineligible for service. According to New York writer Alan Shapiro, of the 27 million men who were of draft age, 8.7 million voluntarily enlisted and 500,000 declared themselves conscientious objectors, went into hiding, or fled to Canada. Some 16 million men avoided military service through a complex SSS classification system of exemptions, deferments, postponements, and disqualifications that many critics say was rigged in favor of the well-connected and the wealthy.

Men in Class II-S, for example, were deferred as long as they remained full-time college students. College enrollment increased sharply among those who could afford a college education, a source of resentment among working-class and poor young men who were not as fortunate. Ministers and divinity students were exempt from the draft; not surprisingly, there was a boom in vocations to the ministry and rabbinate. As more and more army and marine troops were sent to fight on the ground in Vietnam, young men with connections sought service in relatively safe branches such as the Coast

Guard and in National Guard or Reserve units, which had room for only a handful of the applicants trying to get in. Deferments were also allowed for registrants with certain physical or psychological problems, either temporary or permanent, a classification that was notoriously abused by savvy registrants who faked medical or psychological conditions or whose families successfully pressured doctors or draft boards to exempt them on medical grounds. The armed forces officially considered homosexuality a "moral defect," and homosexuals were not permitted to serve in the armed forces in any capacity. Many draftees without student deferments falsely claimed to be gay to avoid induction, but the GLBT Historical Society reports that few deferments based on sexuality were actually granted in the Vietnam War era. The list of deferments goes on: Class II-C, agricultural deferment; Class IV-A, veterans or sole surviving sons; Class III-A, parents.

The SSS assures draft registrants in the early 2000s: "if a draft were held today, it would be dramatically different from the one held during the Vietnam War. A series of reforms during the latter part of the Vietnam conflict changed the way the draft operated to make it more fair and equitable. If a draft were held today, there would be fewer reasons to excuse a man from service." However, a number of deferments—for conscientious objectors, ministers and divinity students, and, for short periods, college students, for example—are still allowed and could be controversial again if the draft is revived. The viewpoints in the following chapter debate who should be subject to and who should be exempt from a fair and equitable draft.

| *"It's time to accept that any future draft must inevitably include women."*

Women Should Be Eligible for the Draft

Philip Gold and Erin Solaro

Seattle-based writers Philip Gold and Erin Solaro oppose rein-stating the draft. However, in the following viewpoint they support full participation of women in the armed services; advocate dropping all restrictions on women's performance of combat duty, including ground combat; they argue that because women bear equal responsibility for the common defense (and the military already is dependent on servicewomen). In the event of a draft, women must be included. Philip Gold, former history professor at Georgetown University, was a senior fellow in national security affairs at the conservative think tank Discovery Institute before his opposition to the Iraq war and the Bush neocon agenda led him to break from conservatism entirely in 2002. He is the author of The Coming Draft: The Crisis in Our Military and Why Selective Service Is Wrong for America. *Erin Solaro traveled to Iraq and Afghanistan in 2004–2005 to research the status of women under arms. She is the author of* Women in the Line of Fire: What You Should Know About Women in the Military.

Philip Gold and Erin Solaro, "America's Volunteer Army Isn't Working, But What Will?" *Seattle Post-Intelligencer*, October 1, 2006. Reproduced by permission of the authors.

As you read, consider the following questions:

1. According to Gold and Solaro, what was the Founding Fathers' original intent for citizen military service, and how would that negate the need for a draft?

2. How should the Universal Militia Act of 1792 be amended, according to the authors?

3. What forms of military service other than the federal armed forces do the authors say should be further opened to women?

Today, the issue of conscription is deader than last week's roadkill. But it will not stay dead much longer. Iraq will continue to fester. Our armed forces are imploding when they should be expanding—the Army and the National Guard, especially. The world is not getting less dangerous. A year or two from now, a disaster or two from now, expect the issue to re-emerge.

Three Bad Options

Expect also to be told that America has only three options: continued reliance on an all-volunteer military; universal national service with "military and non-military options"; or re-institution of some form of direct federal conscription.

All three are militarily unsuitable, politically and culturally unacceptable and morally wrong. Fortunately, there is a fourth option: to return to the Founding Fathers' original intent for citizen military service, then adapt that intent to 21st-century perils.

Pure voluntarism works, at least when it comes to meeting quotas. All you have to do is to pump up the cash and lower the standards. But that's no way to defend a democracy, especially since the quotas are pitifully inadequate to meet present and future needs.

Universal service constitutes little more than state-sanctioned involuntary servitude. It would create a massive teenager-herding bureaucracy and produce mostly resentment, although many liberal proponents admire the old West German system, with conscientious objectors doing the drudge work of their welfare state. As for instilling the "spirit of sacrifice" in our nation's youth, perhaps all that debt we're leaving them constitutes sacrifice enough.

The direct federal draft is arguably unconstitutional. Article I, Section 8 gives Congress the power to "raise Armies"—an 18th-century term for professional volunteer forces. The same article authorizes Congress to "provide for calling forth the Militia (of the states) to execute the Laws of the Union, suppress Insurrections and repel Invasions." By original intent, the federal government may draw upon the people only under certain specified conditions. Overseas wars of choice are not on the list. Had the Founders desired a direct federal draft, they would have authorized one—a fact that, since the Civil War, the Supreme Court has shamefully chosen to explain away or ignore.

A Better, Fourth Option:
Participation by All Americans

But what did the Founders intend? They certainly did not regard the Constitution as a suicide pact, or their list of perils as exhaustive. They also held a high regard for the citizenry in arms.

Specifically, they viewed participation in the common defense as an unalienable obligation and right of citizenship, an obligation and right extending over a lifetime but taking a variety of forms. The Universal Militia Act of 1792 decreed every adult (white male, back then) citizen a member of the "unorganized militia." This law is still on the books as USC (United States Code) Title 10, Section 311. They did this because they conceived of the common defense as a continuum,

Women Should Be Required to Register with the Selective Service

In 1981, the Supreme Court upheld [the Selective Service registration] males-only law as reasonable because there were so many restrictions against women in the military.

But that was [as of 2007, 26] years ago, before women were on the court, before most of the restrictions were lifted, before there were 33 female generals and 212,000 female soldiers doing nearly every job in the military short of ground combat. . . .

Gradually, as the brass found that women can do the job, we ran out of reasons for treating them differently in the military. Why then treat them differently in registering for Selective Service, a list gathered in case of emergency?

Ellen Goodman,
"Why Not Register Women for Future Military Draft?"
Stop the Draft, *January 17, 2003,*
www.stopthedraft.com/index.php?articleID=1483&sectionID=65.

extending from individual and local self-defense and law enforcement to emergencies such as riot and insurrection, with federal foreign war only at the far end. Most of the world still lives that way, with no clear boundaries between threats.

Today, once again, so do we. The global war against terrorism. The travails of the Middle East. Transnational organized crime with political dimensions. Homeland security. Border control. Disaster relief in an age of climate change. Soon enough, the American people will accept that the tidy old divisions of threat and labor no longer avail, and that we can no longer be passive consumers of national security.

We the People must provide for the common defense.

It is time to offer the American people a variety of ways to do so. A few examples:

Individuals could join the active forces as fully deployable volunteers, or as members available for overseas duty only upon declaration of war. There is precedent for this: The 1940 draft restricted draftees to the Western Hemisphere. The Pentagon won't like it, but who's working for whom?

Individuals could serve in the National Guard and service reserves on the same basis, or perhaps rotate between deployable and non-deployable units. Opportunities for individuals with critical skills to serve as specialists should also be enhanced.

Official state militias should be expanded. These organizations, authorized by USC Title 32, Section 309, were created mostly during the world wars, when state Guard forces went overseas. They cannot be federalized. Twenty-four states now maintain such forces. If the National Guard is to maintain its role as a de facto second standing army, the state militias must be enhanced.

Specialized volunteer units, legally chartered and properly trained and supervised, should be formed for everything from border control to disaster relief. These are not "vigilantes." However, not creating such forces may well encourage vigilantism.

In short, when the service debate revives, the fundamental choice should not be federal coercion vs. voluntarism. The debate should include crafting a defense that meets real-world needs across the continuum by offering various forms of participation to every American man.

And woman.

Drop All Restrictions on Women's Service, Including Combat

This isn't the place to recap the history of American feminism, or women's military service. However, American feminism was not always either stridently anti-military or mindlessly anti-violence. Feminism and the women's suffrage movement grew out of the Abolitionist movement. For these feminists, using enormous violence to preserve the Union and abolish slavery was not an issue, even if women's service wasn't on the agenda. Nor should it have been. Early feminists were preoccupied with obtaining property and voting rights for women, in an era when women died wholesale in childbirth, and of complications of pregnancy and childbirth. It would have been wrong to expect women to risk their lives for a state that considered them citizens only for purposes of taxation, and obscene to bear the twin risks of reproduction and combat.

This changed. New generations of feminists opened up education, credit, employment and jury duty, as well as military service, to women. Unfortunately, in the 1960s, feminism conflated itself with the anti-American international peace movement and the "Blame America First" crowd at home. The military seemed not a vital national institution but a bastion of malignant masculinity. Servicewomen were less citizens and patriots than victims and battering rams, useful for cracking (and humiliating) the services. It was a transparent attempt to have equality of rights without equality of responsibility, not least of all because it denied the very concept of citizen military responsibility. And since the Jessica Lynch and Abu Ghraib embarassments [incidents involving the capture and rescue of a U.S. servicewoman and prisoner abuse at the hands of U.S. servicewomen, respectively], what's left of organized feminism has all but ignored the nearly 150,000 servicewomen who have gone to war. For to honor them, they would have to look beyond the present mess and acknowledge that the strength and survival of the American Republic is of vital interest to American women and is in fact worth defending.

It's time for real feminists—those of us who genuinely believe in women's equal responsibility for the world—to recalibrate feminism's relationship to violence and the military. It's time now because, whatever your opinion of Iraq (which both of us opposed since 2002), it's only one campaign in a much larger, longer war in which American women, and the women of the world, have an enormous stake.

Toward that end, the unorganized militia law should be amended to include women. All state militias and such specialized organizations as may be created must be fully open to women. It is time for the federal military to drop all remaining restrictions on women's service, especially in ground combat. This is not about equality for the sake of equality or career opportunities. It is certainly not about quotas; there should be none. It's about the military being honest with women that they will face combat in any future war—and about the fact that women are routinely in combat today. It's also about the fact that the military is now irrevocably dependent on women, who now constitute 15 percent of the force. And it's time to accept that any future draft must inevitably include women. In the past, both Congress and the Supreme Court have deferred to the military's assessment that it didn't need women. This assessment no longer accords with reality.

But will there be a draft? We fervently hope not. The federal government deserves no blank check on the lives of our young. But we also hold that the best way to avoid it, long term, is to resurrect the notion of citizen responsibility for the common defense, as a normal part of a citizen's life. Forms of participation may vary greatly, but the principle is constant. And perhaps one of the greatest contributions that a new civic feminism could make would be to affirm that America has every right to expect her women to defend her.

> *"The answer to the many folks who suggest conscripting women is this: Real Americans don't send women to war. Neither do real men."*

Women Should Not Be Eligible for the Draft

R. Cort Kirkwood

In the following viewpoint, syndicated columnist R. Cort Kirkwood strongly objects to drafting women. The current draft exemption for women is legally tied to their exemption from combat, he reasons, so if the exemption from combat is dropped as many have called for, women should expect to have to register for the draft. Kirkwood opposes both developments. Just because women currently do *fly combat aircraft and serve on combatant ships does not mean they* should, *he argues: Women lack the physical strength to win battles against men, cannot meet the same standards men meet in military training, and should be spared the "carnage and cruelty of war" on moral and religious grounds unless Americans are prepared to accept the brutalization of society. R. Cort Kirkwood is a regular contributor to Lew*

Rockwell.com, a nonprofit news and commentary Web site affiliated with the libertarian Mises Institute in Auburn, Alabama. He served on the Presidential Commission on the Assignment of Women in the Armed Forces, established by George H.W. Bush in 1992.

As you read, consider the following questions:

1. What evidence does Kirkwood offer to support his claim that women lack physical prowess to serve in combat?

2. By how much would the percentage of women in the armed forces drop if women were required to meet the same training standards as male recruits, according to the author?

3. What is the only situation in which Kirkwood says women should be used in combat?

[In 2003] this writer suggested a fine way to stop American wars of conquest: Conscript the sons of politicians and bureaucrats who start them. Nearly three dozen letters came in, almost every one posing this question with the corollary mandate: Why are you excluding the daughters? Let Bush send his daughters to war.

It's a passionate and in some ways understandable reaction.

And most likely, it won't be long before women, along with young men, are required to register for the draft; the explanation for that observation appears below. But first, an answer for those correspondents: The debate over women in combat turns on two questions: whether women can do it (handle the rigors of combat) and whether they should do it (is it morally acceptable and socially desirable).

In a word, no. It is un-American, un-Christian, and immoral.

Women Lack Necessary Physical Prowess

As a practical matter, 99 percent of women are unsuited for combat, and that includes flying combat aircraft and serving on combatant ships. That women do these things doesn't mean they should; it just means the military has been feminized and civilianized, as any military man will admit after a few shots of Jack Daniels at the Officers' Club, and of course, after his commanding officer leaves.

In the early 1990s, I was a staff member on the Presidential Commission on the Assignment of Women in the Armed Forces. The evidence the commission gathered was clear on one thing: Women don't belong in combat.

The evidence showed women lack the necessary physical prowess. The strongest woman recruit, generally, is only as strong as the weakest man. Given that the services try to weed out the weakest men, it's counterproductive to recruit even the strongest women. And our volunteer military, remember, doesn't get the strongest women; it gets average women.

As well, women suffer higher rates of bone fractures, and other factors such as menstruation, pregnancy and aging militate against recruiting women as combat soldiers. The 20-something woman, for instance, has about the same lung-power as the 50-something man.

Well, that might be true for ground combat, the feminists insist, but surely they can fly jets and bombers. It's all just a Nintendo game up there. Again, untrue. Flying high-performance jets requires incredible conditioning and strength, particularly in the neck. Top Gun fighter pilots told the commission (and news reports later confirmed) that unqualified lady pilots routinely passed Naval flight training. At that time at least, officers were rated on the number of women they promoted. The result in one case? Kara Hultgreen, the first woman to "qualify" flying an F-14, was killed when her jet crashed because she couldn't land it on the carrier Abraham Lincoln.

But let's suppose women fly jets as well as men. What happens when one is shot down? The safety of the high-tech cockpit is gone, and she is alone on the ground, trying to survive. . . .

As for the ships, consider the obvious: You don't send a few nubile sailorettes aboard Navy ships with 1,500 horny sailors, no matter what the Navy says about its "leadership" correcting carnal temptations. As well, the strength deficit surfaces again in many shipboard tasks too numerous to mention here.

Women Cannot Meet Training Standards

Military training is another area where the women fall flat; they cannot survive the same basic training as men, so it is "gender-normed." That means the services (and military academies) have different standards for women than for men, and not just for hair length. If women were held to the same standards as men, more than 14 percent of our armed forces would not be women; they could not attend the academies. Oddly enough, the feminists aver that scrapping the double standard would be discriminatory! So much for judging someone on her true merit.

In the decade since the commission heard tons of testimony on these points, nothing has changed unless women have evolved markedly improved muscle and bone.

In reply to these unassailable facts, some suggest some women can meet the same standards with the proper weight training and physical-fitness regimen. That's a stretch, but let's say a few can. That takes us back to the weakest man vs. the strongest woman. What standard would these few meet? The lowest among the men? Even if they fell among men of medium strength, consider the prohibitive cost of selecting these Amazonian anomalies from among general population. And finding them assumes they want to be found.

Congress Upholds Male-Only Draft Registration

In a report accompanying the National Defense Authorization Act for Fiscal Year 1994, which repealed some of the statutory bars to women in combat, the House Armed Services Committee noted that the decision to lift those prohibitions should not *"be construed as tacit committee concurrence in an expansion of the assignment of women to units or positions whose mission requires routine engagement in direct combat on the ground, or be seen as a suggestion that Selective Service registration or conscription include women."*

Center for Military Readiness, "Court Dismisses Lawsuit to Include Women in Draft Registration," September 4, 2003.

A friend of mine, a former Green Beret, suggests an experiment: Let's train two squads, one all women, the other all men, to peak physical and combat-ready condition. Then drop them in the woods for a war game and see who wins.

Point is, women get by in the military only because of men. . . . [Few women] have the strength to carry a fallen 200-pound comrade out of harm's way. Forgetting about combat, some women aircraft mechanics need men to lift their toolboxes. Without men, the armed forces would collapse, and the more women the military enlists, the weaker it becomes.

As one commissioner remarked in exasperation: "Women are not little men, and men are not big women."

The Moral Question of Women in Combat

That leaves the moral and social questions, which commission member and Vietnam War hero Ron Ray addressed with this remark: "The question isn't whether women can do, it's whether they should do it."

Women should only be used in combat, Ray argued, if national survival demands it; i.e., when the Indians are circling the ranch and the men are dead and wounded. Even then, using women would be a last resort. It would not become a policy. Such an emergency isn't likely to happen here unless Saddam Hussein's vaunted Republican Guards make a spectacular comeback. . . . In that case, we know all the women will be fighting.

The moral and social argument is one of "rights" vs. what is right. The feminists claim combat service is a "right." Nonsense.

A battlefield is not a boardroom, a courtroom or an operating room, and the contrary notion is hyperegalitarianism rooted in feminist fantasies that women "will have made it" when they have commanded troops in battle. Women do not have a "right" to serve. Military service for volunteers is a privilege; for draftees, it is a duty. No one has a "right" to serve, a civilian idea equivalent to having the "right" to be a doctor or lawyer that has no place in the military, whose principal purpose is to kill the enemy and destroy his capacity to fight.

In *Crimson Tide*, Gene Hackman's submarine skipper explained the point: The armed forces defend democracy, they do not practice it.

So much for "rights." Now, as to whether women in combat is right:

At one commission hearing, Col. John Ripley, one of the most famous Marines who fought in Vietnam, explained combat for the largely civilian audience. A good picture of real combat, he said, is walking down a path to find your best friend nailed to a tree, or his private parts in his mouth. The feminists and military women in the audience gnashed their teeth.

Then again, they don't understand that until Bill Clinton's war minister Les Aspin changed it, the law excluding women from combat was always considered a privileged exemption, not sex discrimination. It was the thoughtful recognition that women should be spared the carnage and cruelty of war.

Why Spare Women the Carnage and Cruelty of War?

Why?

Because turning a woman into the kind of person who views such gore without blinking an eye, or who participates in the wanton killing war requires, is a step down to pagan barbarism and cultural suicide. In some sense, given what we've seen in the Gulf, we've already taken that step. But the feminists won't quit until they get women into ground combat units. As recent events prove, no one seems to care what all this means not only culturally but also psychologically.

It will require training men and women to regard the brutalization of women, and a woman's brutalization of others, as normal and acceptable. To train the men properly, a woman commissioner observed, we must erase everything their mothers taught them about chivalry; i.e., that a real man protects a woman from harm. Instead, they must be trained to brain a woman with a pugil stick in training. This truth raises two paradoxes.

On one hand, to completely desensitize the men, such training would be required. But the feminists don't want that because women can't meet the same standards as men; they won't survive it. Yet how are these women to survive combat if they cannot survive real, not gender-normed, basic training? The men would have to protect them. Successfully integrating women in combat means this: A soldier must ignore the screams of a woman POW being tortured and raped.

On the other hand, while the feminists never stop the finger-wagging about "domestic abuse," they importune us to inure men to the wartime abuse of women. Again, to some degree, we're already there. The capture and torture of [Pfc.]

Jessica Lynch and Shoshana Johnson, the single mother, was just another day in the war. But then again, the society that sent these young women to war is the same one that has steroidally-fortified men and women bashing each other senseless in television's faux wrestling, which presents the illusion that women really can fight against men, as well as preposterous movies about women Navy SEALS, or women who receive the Medal of Honor while the men cower in fear.

Lastly, assigning women to combat, or even combat support units like the 507th, purposely subjects them to trials and tribulations for which nature has not prepared them. Such assignments endanger not only the women but also the men around them, who will redirect their attention from fighting toward protecting or helping the women. Men will do that because they are men, because regardless of feminist propaganda, good parents teach their sons about chivalry and honor. The Steinem brigade [reference to followers of feminist Gloria Steinem] doesn't like it, but it's true nonetheless. Thus, men will die unnecessarily. That is immoral and unjust, as is ordering married men and women to live in close quarters where they are tempted to adultery. Some observers even question the legality of orders sending women into combat. But that is a debate for another day.

Ray's point? Civilized Christians don't send women and mothers to fight the wars. *Chronicles* editor Tom Fleming has observed that our nation has become anti-Christian. The saga of [captured service women] and other military women proves him right.

The Final Answer

Back to that draft.

Don't be surprised if women are required to register. Legally speaking, the draft exemption for women is tied to their exemption from combat. Now women serve in aerial and naval action. And given the proximity to combat of women in "maintenance" and other units, it won't be long before the politicians, and bemedaled generals in the Army and Marines, hoist the white flag and put women in ground combat. Then, some young man will file the inevitable "equal protection" lawsuit and the exemption will fall, its legal rationale having been dropped.

Oddly enough, the silly clamor for women in combat assumes most military women want combat assignments. The commission found that they don't. Only a few aging feminists do, and of course, they won't be subject to the combat assignments or the draft. When you join the military, you join voluntarily, but you go where they need you. When women get their "right" to fight, they won't have the "right" to refuse. And why would they? After that, again, comes the draft for women.

The answer to the many folks who suggest conscripting women is this: Real Americans don't send women to war. Neither do real men.

> "I now believe that if gay men and lesbians served openly in the United States military, they would not undermine the efficacy of the armed forces."

The Military Should Accept Open Homosexuals

John M. Shalikashvili

In the following viewpoint, retired army general John M. Shalikashvili reverses himself on the issue of gays in the military. Shalikashvili was a vocal advocate of the "Don't Ask, Don't Tell" policy established by President Bill Clinton in 1993. In this departure from the existing complete ban on homosexuality, as long as homosexuals hide and do not speak about their sexual orientation and relationships, they may serve in the military and commanders may not investigate their sexuality. Fourteen years later, however, Shalikashvili argues that conservative attitudes within the military have changed, gay and bisexual soldiers are now accepted, and secrecy is no longer needed to preserve unit cohesiveness and effectiveness. John M. Shalikashvili was chairman of the Joint Chiefs of Staff from 1993 to 1997.

John M. Shalikashvili, "Second Thoughts on Gays in the Military," *New York Times*, January 2, 2007. Copyright © 2007 by The New York Times Company. Reprinted with permission.

As you read, consider the following questions:

1. Why did President Bill Clinton initiate Don't Ask, Don't Tell instead of making good on his campaign promise to lift the ban on gays in the military, according to Shalikashvili?

2. According to the Zogby poll cited by the author, what percentage of service members say they are comfortable interacting with gay people?

3. How many foreign nations let gays serve openly without morale or recruitment problems, according to Shalikashvili?

[In December 2006] President [George W.] Bush called for a long-term plan to increase the size of the armed forces. As our leaders consider various options for carrying out Mr. Bush's vision, one issue likely to generate fierce debate is "don't ask, don't tell," the policy that bars openly gay service members from the military. Indeed, leaders in the new Congress are planning to re-introduce a bill to repeal the policy next year.

As was the case in 1993—the last time the American people thoroughly debated the question of whether openly gay men and lesbians should serve in the military—the issue will give rise to passionate feelings on both sides. The debate must be conducted with sensitivity, but it must also consider the evidence that has emerged over the last 14 years.

"Don't Ask, Don't Tell" Was Necessary in 1993

When I was chairman of the Joint Chiefs of Staff, I supported the current policy because I believed that implementing a change in the rules at that time would have been too burdensome for our troops and commanders. I still believe that to have been true. The concern among many in the military was

The Military Rank-and-File Say Gays Should Be Allowed to Serve

A [December 2006] Zogby poll of more than 500 veterans of the Afghanistani and Iraqi conflict [showed] 75 percent of those sampled described themselves as comfortable serving with gays. Almost a quarter of the same group said they knew of a gay member in their very own unit, with two-thirds claiming that this situation had no effect on "personal or unit morale." In Britain and Israel, two of the many nations that already allow open homosexuals to enlist, little impact has been imported.

Chicago Maroon,
"What Justification Is Left for 'Don't Ask, Don't Tell,"
Servicemembers Legal Defense Network, *January 9, 2007.*

that given the longstanding view that homosexuality was incompatible with service, letting people who were openly gay serve would lower morale, harm recruitment and undermine unit cohesion.

In the early 1990s, large numbers of military personnel were opposed to letting openly gay men and lesbians serve. President Bill Clinton, who promised to lift the ban during his campaign, was overwhelmed by the strength of the opposition, which threatened to overturn any executive action he might take. The compromise that came to be known as "don't ask, don't tell" was thus a useful speed bump that allowed temperatures to cool for a period of time while the culture continued to evolve.

The question before us now is whether enough time has gone by to give this policy serious reconsideration. Much evidence suggests that it has.

"Don't Ask, Don't Tell" Is Not Necessary in 2007

Last year [2006] I held a number of meetings with gay soldiers and marines, including some with combat experience in Iraq, and an openly gay senior sailor who was serving effectively as a member of a nuclear submarine crew. These conversations showed me just how much the military has changed, and that gays and lesbians can be accepted by their peers.

This perception is supported by a new Zogby poll of more than 500 service members returning from Afghanistan and Iraq, three quarters of whom said they were comfortable interacting with gay people. And 24 foreign nations, including Israel, Britain and other allies in the fight against terrorism, let gays serve openly, with none reporting morale or recruitment problems.

I now believe that if gay men and lesbians served openly in the United States military, they would not undermine the efficacy of the armed forces. Our military has been stretched thin by our deployments in the Middle East, and we must welcome the service of any American who is willing and able to do the job.

But if America is ready for a military policy of nondiscrimination based on sexual orientation, the timing of the change should be carefully considered. As the 110th Congress opens for business, some of its most urgent priorities, like developing a more effective strategy in Iraq, share widespread support that spans political affiliations. Addressing such issues could help heal the divisions that cleave our country. Fighting early in this Congress to lift the ban on openly gay service members is not likely to add to that healing, and it risks alienating people whose support is needed to get this country on the right track.

By taking a measured, prudent approach to change, political and military leaders can focus on solving the nation's most pressing problems while remaining genuinely open to the eventual and inevitable lifting of the ban. When that day comes, gay men and lesbians will no longer have to conceal who they are, and the military will no longer need to sacrifice those whose service it cannot afford to lose.

> *"It's no secret that our current military leadership . . . continues to overwhelmingly oppose allowing openly homosexual men and women to enlist."*

The Military Should Not Accept Open Homosexuals

J. Matt Barber

J. Matt Barber is policy director for cultural issues for Concerned Women for America, a conservative Christian political-action organization based in Washington, D.C. In the following viewpoint, Barber portrays the movement to drop the ban on open homosexuals in the military as liberal hypocrisy: Politicians pushing a liberal social agenda, such as Speaker of the House Nancy Pelosi, are lobbying to allow gays in the military and boost troop enlistment at the same time they oppose troop surges and escalated deployment to Iraq, he says. Nothing the pro-homosexual lobby says, Barber warns, can change the facts that anti-gay sentiment remains very strong within the military, and homosexuality remains immoral.

J. Matt Barber, "'Gays' in the Military—a Troop 'Surge' Liberals Support," *Concerned Women for America*, January 11, 2007. Reproduced by permission.

As you read, consider the following questions:

1. What organizations does the author claim are behind the campaign to lift the ban on openly gay people serving in the U.S. armed forces?

2. According to Barber, what is the flimsy basis of retired Joint Chiefs of Staff chairman John Shalikashvili's opinion that gays are now well tolerated in the military ranks?

3. How will the Military Readiness Enhancement Act (repealing the Don't Ask, Don't Tell policy) be defeated, in Barber's opinion?

L iberals in Washington are very vocal in opposition to the president's planned deployment of additional troops to the Iraqi theatre, but in the culture war on the home front, those same liberals are prepared to enthusiastically push for an "escalation" in troop enlistment by repealing the military's "don't ask, don't tell" policy and permitting openly homosexual men and women to sign up. (Move over National Guard and Green Berets—make way for the avant-garde and Lavender Berets.)

The Servicemembers Legal Defense Network, the Human Rights Campaign, and a host of other powerful and extremely well-funded pro-homosexual activist groups are leading the charge. But it's the new Speaker of the House, Nancy Pelosi (D-California.), who's sounding the shrill bugle call.

According to the *Washington Blade*, a top "gay" publication, Pelosi has signed on to the homosexual lobby's top-ten "gay" wish-list as a "co-sponsor for all 10 gay- and AIDS-related bills that are languishing in Congress." Of those ten bills, the innocuously titled "Military Readiness Enhancement Act"—which would repeal "don't ask, don't tell"—is a top priority.

Other liberals are weighing in as well. On January 2nd, the *New York Times* fired off a real opinion piece dud. "Second

The Military Rank-and-File Say Gays Should Not Be Allowed to Serve

In December 2006 ... Zogby International released a poll that was commissioned by the Center for the Study of Sexual Minorities in the Military, a gay activist group now called the Michael D. Palm Center. The Zogby news release publicized an innocuous question about respondents' relative "comfort" with homosexuals, but omitted mention of the key question displayed on the pollster's website: "*Do you agree or disagree with allowing gays and lesbians to serve openly in the military?*"

On that question, 26% of respondents agreed, but 37% disagreed. The poll also found that 32% of respondents were "Neutral," and 5% were "Not sure." The combined 69% who were opposed or neutral outnumbered the 26% who wanted the law repealed. This was hardly a mandate for radical change.

Elaine Donnelly, "General Pace and the PC Police," Center for Military Readiness, March 26, 2007.

Thoughts on Gays in the Military" was penned by blast from the past, John Shalikashvili, chairman of the Joint Chiefs of Staff under the Clinton administration. Needless to say, Shalikashvili's column sorely missed its target.

In the piece, Shalikashvili opines that "don't ask, don't tell" has outlived its usefulness and that it was only "a useful speed bump that allowed temperatures to cool for a period of time while the culture continued to evolve."

So, while admonishing us that "the debate must be conducted with sensitivity," Shalikashvili not so gingerly implies that those of us in the majority—those of us who still believe that it's ill-advised to engage in radical social experimentation within the ranks of a military immersed in the War on Terror—are a bunch of knuckle-dragging Neanderthals stuck in the primordial sludge of the "homophobic" 1990s.

Shalikashvili notes that: "The concern among many in the military was that . . . letting people who were openly gay serve would lower morale, harm recruitment and undermine unit cohesion." Well sir, that's still the concern "among many in the military" today—most in fact—and those concerns are just as well founded now, as they were during the military's Paleolithic Clintonian era.

Anti-Gay Attitudes Have Not Changed and Will Not Change

It's no secret that our current military leadership, as they've done throughout this liberally manufactured debate, continues to overwhelmingly oppose allowing openly homosexual men and women to enlist. And Shalikashvili fails to provide any evidence whatsoever which would support his pro-homosexual contention to the contrary (other than perhaps his own "evolving" moral compass). He offers no evidence which would indicate that *anything* has changed or that it ever *will* change.

In fact, one of the scant few pieces of anecdotal evidence Shalikashvili offers up in attempts to bolster his argument, has the unintended result of causing both hemispheres of your brain to abruptly and violently swap places.

While gathering support for his assertion that it's now time, and "equality" dictates that openly "gay" sailors be permitted to serve as effective members of, say, a nuclear submarine crew, Shalikashvili cheerfully informs us that he's had his opinion seconded by "an openly gay senior sailor who was serving effectively as a member of a nuclear submarine crew." He's asking for permission to eat that omelet—but already has an empty plate in front of him and egg on his face.

So, as Shalikashvili, Pelosi and other proponents of the "gays in the military" social experiment prepare to ramp up efforts to inject their San Francisco brand of moral relativism into a last sound vestige of a morally misguided and politically correct society, one can only hope that good old fashioned common sense will prevail.

And while the 110th Congress gets revved up, and our fighting men and women face possible cutbacks in funding and other threatened roadblocks in their ability to execute the War on Terror, it would be shameful if they additionally had to brace themselves to absorb the destructive impact of leftist social experiments gone awry.

Regrettably, however, it looks like our armed services are going have to rely on their last line of defense on this one. When the "Military Readiness Enhancement Act" makes its way to the Oval Office, as it likely will in fairly short order, we can only hope that President [George W.] Bush will bring us all back down to earth for a while by demonstrating once again that the veto pen is mightier than the PC sword.

> *"In the event of a draft, the [Selective Service System] will conduct a national lottery to determine the order in which registered men are called up."*

Draftees Should Be Selected by Lottery

Alliance for Security

The Alliance for Security is affiliated with the Washington, D.C.-based organization Vietnam Veterans for America, both founded by Vietnam veteran and activist Bobby Muller. In the following viewpoint, the alliance reports that the Selective Service System (SSS) is ready to reinstate and implement a revamped military draft as soon as it receives orders from the president. The coming draft, he argues, will have fewer loopholes that allow the rich and powerful to avoid conscription compared with its Vietnam-era counterpart, but it will still involve selection by lottery. As of 2007, all males between the ages of 18 and 25 are required to register for the draft; from this pool, a lottery based on year and date of birth is the fairest way to pull conscripts' names and supply manpower for the armed forces in the event of national emergency.

"Draft 101: What It Is and How It Would Work," *Alliance for Security*, 2004. Reproduced by permission.

As you read, consider the following questions:

1. How many American men were drafted during World Wars I and II, the Korean War, and the Vietnam conflict, according to the author?
2. How will a new draft lottery close the student-deferment loophole, according to the Alliance for Security?
3. According to the SSS lottery described by the Alliance for Security, who will be drafted first and how will subsequent draftees be chosen?

Yes, that's right. We're talking about military conscription, otherwise known as The Draft. While many people may think of the draft as a relic of the Vietnam War era, in fact, a debate is brewing about whether or not conscription will become necessary in light of current and potential military commitments around the world. At the same time, the federal agency created in the 1940s to coordinate the draft remains in place today and is continually preparing to reinstate a conscription process.

The Selective Service System (SSS) is an independent agency within the executive branch of the U.S. government. Its mission is to provide manpower to the armed forces in a national emergency and, should there be a draft, run an Alternative Service Program for people classified as conscientious objectors. Together with its volunteer draft boards, the SSS stands ready to implement a draft as soon as it receives an order from the President.

A Little History

The history of conscription in this country dates back to the Revolutionary War. It was not until World War I, when President Woodrow Wilson signed into law the Selective Service Act of 1917, that the United States military came to depend mainly upon draftees to fight its wars. During that conflict, the Selective Service drafted more than 2.8 million men, who accounted for 78 percent of the country's fighting force. The draft ended along with the war in 1918. President [Franklin D.] Roosevelt established the country's first "peacetime draft" (World War II was well underway, but the U.S. had not yet entered it) when he signed into law the Selective Training and Service Act of 1940 following the fall of France to the Nazis. This law gave birth to the Selective Service System as an independent agency reporting to the President. Ultimately, the Selective Service drafted more than 10 million men during World War II.

The draft remained in place at the end of WWII and, except for a brief period in 1947–48 when the draft was suspended, the government used conscription to fill vacancies in the military during times of conflict and relative peace throughout the Cold War era. The U.S. conscripted more than 1.5 million people during the Korean War and over 1.8 million during the Vietnam conflict. Although draftees comprised only 16 percent of the armed forces in Vietnam, they accounted for more than half the Army's battle deaths. These casualties, in turn, fell disproportionately on the working class and African Americans. The draft grew increasingly unpopular, causing President [Richard M.] Nixon to phase it out. Conscription ended in 1973; two years later President Ford did away with mandatory registration. However, in 1980 President [Jimmy] Carter reinstated registration due to concerns about Soviet expansionism.

Things Are Different Now

Since 1980, the Selective Service System has been in a holding pattern, updating the plans and systems that would enable it to implement a draft, while at the same time continuing to register draft-age youth. Almost all male citizens and residents of the U.S., ages 18 to 25, are required to register with the Selective Service. Draft-age men with dual citizenship must also sign up, even if they live outside the U.S.

How the Lottery Works

If and when the Congress and the President reinstate a military draft, the Selective Service System would conduct a National Draft Lottery to determine the order in which young men would be drafted.

The lottery would establish the priority of call based on the birth dates of registrants. The first men drafted would be those turning age 20 during the calendar year of the lottery....

To make the lottery as fair as possible, the National Institute of Standards and Technology (NIST) developed a unique random calendar and number selection program for Selective Service. Using this random selection method for birthdays, each day of the year is selected by computer in a random manner, and that date is placed in a capsule. The capsules are then loaded in a large drum on a random basis. By the same method, numbers from 1 to 365 ... are also selected in a random fashion, placed in capsules, and the capsules are placed into a second drum....

Here is how the lottery would work: One capsule is drawn from the drum containing birth dates January 1 through December 31. One capsule is then drawn from the drum containing the sequence numbers from 1 through 365 ... and the date and number are paired to establish the sequence number for each birth date....

For example, if the date of August 4 is drawn first from the "date" drum, and the sequence number of 32 is drawn from the "number's" drum at the same time, then those men turning 20 on August 4 would be ordered for induction processing only after men whose birthdays drew sequence numbers 1 through 31. The drawings continue until all 365 ... birthdays of the year are paired with a sequence number.

Selective Service System, "Selective Service Lottery: Fast Facts,"
2007, www.sss.gov/fslottery.htm.

Sources agree that a draft today would look very different than during the Vietnam era. In general, there would be fewer exemptions. For instance, in the past, full-time students making progress toward a degree qualified for deferment; under current law, students could defer only until the end of the current semester. Many people believe that, if a draft took place today, women would be included. The possibility of drafting women is revisited periodically as women's role in the military evolves. Congress would have to legislate such a measure, but the SSS has the capability to execute such a mission should it be instructed to do so.

Some experts believe that prior to, or instead of, instituting a full-scale general draft, the Selective Service might be called upon to implement a draft of people with specialized skills. The SSS, itself, has stated that a draft targeting linguists, computer experts, and medical personnel is more likely than a general draft and has focused much of its planning on preparing for such an effort.

From Your Couch to Boot Camp: How a Draft Would Work

Current regulations dictate that the Selective Service must deliver the first inductees to the military within 193 days of receiving a request from the President to activate a draft. Here's an overview of what the process would look like for a general draft:

1. **Authorization.** The first step is for Congress to pass legislation authorizing a draft. The President must then sign the bill into law and give an order to the SSS to implement a draft. This process could take as little as two days.

2. **Lottery.** While all men between the ages of 18 and 25 are required to register for the draft, the military would not need nearly as many men as fall into

that age range. Therefore, in the event of a draft, the SSS will conduct a national lottery to determine the order in which registered men are called up. Men who turn twenty during the calendar year in which the draft occurs will be the first called. The lottery determines the order of birth dates to be called up. Once all eligible twenty-year-olds have been called, then the process moves on to 21-, 22-, 23-, 24-, and 25-year-olds, respectively. According to the Selective Service, it is unlikely that 18- and 19-year-olds would be drafted. As of the first of January in the year of his 21st birthday, a potential draftee drops down to the second level of priority, in the year of his 22nd birthday to the third level, and so on.

3. **Full Mobilization of SSS**. Meanwhile, the Selective Service will fully mobilize, calling up its 56 State Directors (one for each state and one each for Guam, Puerto Rico, North Mariana Islands, Virgin Islands, Washington, D.C., and New York City) and 350 Reserve Officers for full-time duty. Approximately 2,000 draft and appeal boards staffed by roughly 11,000 volunteers will also spring into action.

4. **Notification and Evaluation**. Men whose birth dates have the lowest lottery numbers will receive induction notices that tell them which area SSS offices and local draft boards will handle their cases. The notice will also provide them information on where to report for an examination. All selected registrants must undergo physical, psychological, mental and moral evaluations. After undergoing this evaluation, those men declared "fit for service" have ten days to file for exemption, postponement, or deferment.

5. **Processing and Induction.** Local draft boards review requests for exemptions, postponements and deferments and classify people, either identifying them as eligible for induction or eligible for an exemption, postponement, or deferment. Conscientious objectors may be allowed to perform alternative service or to perform non-combat service within the military. Ministers of religion are currently considered eligible for exemption, and ministerial students may receive a deferral. People may also submit a claim for deferment if they believe their induction would subject their families to significant hardship.

6. **Training and Deployment.** Of course, for those who receive induction notices, the process is just beginning. All inductees must report to a "Military Entrance Processing Station" in their area within ten days of receiving an induction notice. They will then be placed in basic training. Inductees will receive at least three to six months of training before being deployed to a combat zone. Some inductees might receive more extensive training in a specialized field, which could last as much as a year or more. However, given that draftees are expected to serve 24 months, it is unlikely that the military would spend significant amounts of time providing specialized training to large numbers of conscripts.

> *"While a conventional draft may never be needed, a draft of men and women possessing . . . critical skills may be warranted in a future crisis, if too few volunteer."*

Draftees Could Be Selected for Critical, Specialized Skills

Charles S. Abell et al.

Charles S. Abell was principal deputy undersecretary of defense for personnel and readiness in the Department of Defense in 2003. In the following viewpoint, Abell and other officials in the Department of Defense and Selective Service System (SSS) argue that although there is sufficient fighting capability in the all-volunteer army to counter threats to national security, there are known shortages of military personnel with certain critical skills, and a selective draft of highly skilled people may be the best way to supply military manpower in a national emergency. In Abell's view, an inventory of individuals' training and skills, collected at the time of draft registration from women as well as men, would be useful to several government agencies concerned with national security, including the Department of Defense, the Department of Homeland Security, and the Public Health Service.

Charles S. Abell et al., "Topical Agenda: The Department of Defense (Personnel & Readiness) and the Selective Service System," *Selective Service System memo*, February 11, 2003, pp. 5–6.

As you read, consider the following questions:

1. What information is currently required for Selective Service registration, according to Abell et al.

2. What additional information do the authors suggest should be collected from men and women when they register for the draft?

3. How do the authors propose to update the critical skills inventory over time?

With known shortages of military personnel with certain critical skills, and with the need for the nation to be capable of responding to domestic emergencies as a part of Homeland Security planning, changes should be made in the Selective Service System's registration, program and primary mission.

Critical Shortages in Specialized Skills

Currently, and in accordance with the Military Selective Service Act (MSSA) [50 U.S.C., App. 451 et seq.], the Selective Service System (SSS) collects and maintains personal information from all U.S. male citizens and resident aliens. Under this process, each man is required to "present himself for and submit to registration" upon reaching age 18. The methods by which a man can register with Selective Service include the Internet, mail-back postcard, checking a box on other government forms, and through the driver's license applications process in many states. The collected data is retained in an active computer file until the man reaches age 26 and is no longer draft eligible. It consists of the man's name, address, Social Security number, and date of birth. Currently, 91 percent of all men, ages 18 through 25, are registered, enabling the SSS to conduct a timely, fair. and equitable draft in the event the Congress and the President decide to reinstate conscription during a crisis.

Preparations for a Skills Draft Are Underway

[On] **October 19, 2004,** an article in the *New York Times* titled "U.S. Has Contingency Plans for a Draft of Medical Workers" appear[ed], revealing that Widemeyer Communications was hired during the summer to help the SSS [Selective Service System] prepare an enormous draft of doctors, nurses, and 61 medical specialties. What is not mentioned is that the Medical Draft will be expanded to include medical equipment repairpersons and even medical form processors. **SSS spokesman [Richard] Flavahan says that 36,000 doctors and nurses, more than 1% of the total 3.4 million men and women in the U.S. under the age of 44, are planned to be inducted in the first batch** once the Skills Draft is activated, showing the current great need or possibly a future need from new invasions and conquests.

"Can You Afford to Believe Bush and the Republicans on the Draft?" The Blatant Truth, *January 30, 2005,* *http://blatanttruth.org/draft.php.*

However, the Secretary of Defense and Department of Defense manpower officials have stated recently [as of February 2003] that a draft will not be necessary for any foreseeable crisis. They assume that sufficient fighting capability exists in today's "all-volunteer" active and reserve Armed Forces for likely contingencies, making a conventional draft of untrained manpower somewhat obsolete. Yet, Defense manpower officials conceded there are critical shortages of military personnel with certain special skills, such as medical personnel, linguists, computer network engineers, etc. The costs of attracting and retaining such personnel for military service could be prohibitive, leading some officials to conclude that while a conventional draft may never be needed, a draft of men and women possessing these critical skills may be warranted in a future crisis, if too few volunteer.

Change Draft Registration to ID Desirable Draftees

In line with today's needs, the SSS' structure, programs and activities should be re-engineered toward maintaining a national inventory of American men and (for the first time) women, ages 18 through 34, with an added focus on identifying individuals with critical skills.

An interagency task force should examine the feasibility of this proposal which would require amendments to the MSSA, expansion of the current registration program, and inclusion of women. In addition to the basic identifying information collected in the current program, the expanded and revised program would require all registrants to indicate whether they have been trained in, possess, and professionally practice, one or more skills critical to national security or community health and safety. This could take the form of an initial "self-declaration" as a part of the registration process. Men and women would enter on the SSS registration form a multi-digit number representing their specific critical skill (e.g., similar to military occupational specialty or Armed Forces Specialty Code with Skill Identifier), taken from a lengthy list of skills to be compiled and published by the Departments of Defense and Homeland Security. Individuals proficient in more than one critical skill would list the practiced skill in which they have the greatest degree of experience and competency. They would also be required to update reported information as necessary until they reach age 35. This unique data base would provide the military (and national, state, and municipal government agencies) with immediately available links to vital human resources. . .in effect, a single, most accurate and complete, national inventory of young Americans with special skills.

While the data base's "worst-case" use might be to draft such personnel into military or homeland security assignments during a national mobilization, its very practical peacetime use could be to support recruiting and direct marketing campaigns aimed at encouraging skilled personnel to volunteer for community or military service opportunities, and to consider applying for hard-to-fill public sector jobs. Local government agencies could also lap this data base to locate nearby specialists for help with domestic crises and emergency situations.

With the changes described above, SSS programs would be modified to serve the contemporary needs of several customers. Department of Defense, Department of Homeland Security (FEMA, U.S. Border Patrol, U.S. Customs, INS), Corporation for National Service, Public Health Service, and other federal and state agencies seeking personnel with critical skills for national security or community service assignments. The SSS would thus play a more vital, relevant, and immediate role in shoring up America's strength and readiness in peace and war.

Periodical Bibliography

The following articles have been selected to supplement the diverse views presented in this chapter.

Lizette Alvarez — "Women at War," *New York Times Upfront*, March 12, 2007.

David F. Burrelli — "Homosexuals and U.S. Military Policy: Current Issues," *CRS Report for Congress, Congressional Research Service*, May 27, 2005.

Nathaniel Frank — "Revolving Door for Troops," *The Washington Post*, July 12, 2004.

Stan Goff — "Will the U.S. Re-Open the Draft?" *From the Wilderness*, 2004, www.fromthewilderness.com/free/ww3/022704_draft_goff.html.

LD Resources — "Should a Learning Disability Be a Military Draft Exemption?" April 26, 2005, www.ldresources.org/?p=940.

Martha McSally — "Women in Combat: Is the Current Policy Obsolete?" *Duke Journal of Gender Law & Policy*, May 2007.

New American — "Draft Registration for 15-Year-Olds?" December 13, 2004.

New American — "Momentum Builds for Drafting Women," May 31, 2004.

Robert Pear — "U.S. Has Contingency Plans for a Draft of Medical Workers," *New York Times*, October 19, 2004.

John Van Doorn — "Raise the Fighting Age," *North County Times (San Diego)*, May 29, 2007.

John Zogby et al. — "Opinions of Military Personnel on Sexual Minorities in the Military," Zoby International, *Michael D. Palm Center*, December 2006.

CHAPTER 4

Should Alternatives to the Military Draft Be Pursued?

Chapter Preface

In 2001 Secretary of Defense Donald Rumsfeld promised to overhaul the Pentagon and transform the U.S. military into a "leaner" force with a "small footprint" that relied more on covert operations, sophisticated weapons systems, and private contractors. By the time Rumsfeld left the Bush cabinet in November 2006, the armed forces were employing private contractors on an unprecedented scale in every aspect of military operations, including combat, and military contractors had been formally designated as an integral component of the army's warfighting capability. As of 2007, an estimated one hundred thousand private contractors, many armed, are on the ground in Iraq. Their vast array of duties include everything from food service to defense training and providing security for U.S. diplomats, nongovernmental organizations such as the Red Cross, and engineering firms that need protection in high-risk conflict areas.

Perhaps the most powerful private contractor is Blackwater USA, characterized by investigative reporter Jeremy Scahill as "a shadowy mercenary company" that amounts to "a politically connected private army." According to Scahill, Blackwater "has 2,300 personnel deployed in nine countries, with twenty thousand other contractors at the ready. It has a fleet of more than twenty aircraft, including helicopter gunships and a private intelligence division, and it is manufacturing surveillance blimps and target systems." By hiring private contractors such as Blackwater, the military is under less pressure to revive the military draft and ostensibly saves the government the costs of facilities, personnel training, and supplies. As Blackwater founder Erik Prince claims, Pentagon officials "want to add thirty thousand people [for] costs of anywhere from $3.6 billion to $4 billion. . . . By my math, that comes out to about $135,000 per soldier. We could certainly do it cheaper."

Hiring private security firms also puts willing mercenaries, not U.S. soldiers, in harm's way. As of December 31, 2006, 770 private contractors had been killed in Iraq and 7,761 injured. (In one well-known incident, four Blackwater contractors were ambushed and killed, their bodies desecrated, by Sunni insurgents in Fallujah in 2004, an incident blamed for intensifying Iraqi resistance to the U.S. occupation of Iraq.) And private contractors have been a versatile complement to National Guard units in homeland security and disaster-response operations such as in New Orleans in the aftermath of Hurricane Katrina in 2005.

But the advantages of private military contractors are offset by several serious, and increasingly worrisome, disadvantages. First is the lack of accountability and oversight. Private security firms under contract to the military are immune from civilian lawsuits for their actions, just like the military, but unlike the army they are not bound by military codes or courts of justice. Outside the military chain of command, private contractors can walk away from situations they deem too dangerous and owe no loyalty to military commanders.

A second problem is that Blackwater and other private contractors have been awarded huge military contracts, many on a no-bid basis—$1 billion to Blackwater, $4 billion altogether since the early stages of U.S. operations in Afghanistan—and have been accused of getting away with war profiteering. As of 2007, investigation into Blackwater's Katrina contracts, for example, revealed that the contractor billed the federal government $950 per man per day, for a 600-man force, without having to justify its charges.

Critics of the increased reliance on private contractors cite a third objection: Hiring private contractors, says Michael Ratner, allows the government to fight "wars of aggrandizement, foolish wars and . . . imperialist wars" without citizen resistance. Moreover, contractor deaths are not counted in official casualty totals, masking the true costs of war.

The rise of private contractors such as Blackwater has drawn responses from the flippant ("a coalition of the billing," "rent-an-army," soldiers "going Blackwater") to the fearful (in Scahill's words, "Further privatizing the country's war machine . . . will represent a devastating blow to the future of American democracy") and sparked congressional debate over how such companies should conduct their operations and even whether they should be allowed to exist. The authors of the viewpoints in the following chapter likewise debate the risks and benefits of pursuing this and other alternatives to the military draft.

> "America should move toward a system
> of compulsory, full-time, 18-month ser-
> vice for all able-bodied high school
> graduates."

Universal National Service Should Replace the Selective Service System

William A. Galston

In 1993, Congress passed the National and Community Service Act, fulfilling President Bill Clinton's campaign pledge to expand Americans' opportunities for civilian national service. The act established AmeriCorps, a program in which young Americans volunteer for 10- to 12-month stints in a wide variety of service projects in exchange for educational awards and other benefits. William A. Galston, who participated in the development of the AmeriCorps program, argues in the following viewpoint that a period of universal mandatory national service (including military and civilian options, modeled on AmeriCorps) is all Americans' civic duty and a sound alternative to the draft and the all-volunteer force (AVF). Three decades of the AVF has led to the complacent belief that "being a citizen involves rights without responsibilities," Galston says. Compulsory service would

William A. Galston, *The AmeriCorps Experiment and the Future of National Service.* Washington, DC: Progressive Policy Institute, 2005. Reproduced by permission.

counter that mistaken belief, revitalize citizenship, break down social and class barriers, and amply provide for the nation's defense. William A. Galston is senior fellow in governance studies at the Brookings Institution, a Washington, D.C. think tank, and former Saul Stern Professor of Public Policy at the University of Maryland.

As you read, consider the following questions:

1. In what ways is mandatory national service no different from jury duty, in Galston's view?
2. What objections does the author have to conscription?
3. How does Galston propose to administer a program of universal national service?

America should move toward a system of compulsory, full-time, 18-month service for all able-bodied high school graduates (and in the case of dropouts, all 18-year-olds). They should be allowed to choose between military or civilian service, but if all slots in the military were filled, they would have to perform civilian service. It would cost at least $60 billion per year to fully implement this system, which would certainly slow its development and could well impose a ceiling on participation. A lottery, to which all are exposed and from which none but the unfit can escape, would be the best response to these constraints.

I come to this position via three routes. The first is public service. From 1993 to 1995 I served as deputy assistant to President Clinton for domestic policy, in which capacity I represented the Domestic Policy Council on the task force that was working (against considerable odds) to turn the president's campaign pledge on national service into legislative reality. I believed then, as I do today, that national service can play a key role in revitalizing citizenship. I was dismayed to discover that budgetary pressures, lack of support from some highly placed congressional Democrats, and ideological hostility on the part of right-wing Republicans combined to constrict national service to a fraction of Clinton's original vision. While support for the program has expanded and outright opposition has diminished in the decade since its inception, opportunities to serve are still much less plentiful than they ought to be.

Scholarly research is my second path to universal service. I am a university professor who studies patterns of citizenship and civic engagement, especially among young Americans. Even a casual glance at trends over the past three decades reveals that something has gone awry. While young people are more highly educated than ever and have access to far more information, they tend to know less about their country, pay less attention to news about public affairs, and participate less energetically in political and civic life than did earlier generations of American youth. It is hard to avoid the conclusion that lowered expectations of citizens have contributed to this decline and that higher expectations are part of the solution. Universal service would express, in a particularly vivid and effective way, our collective decision to reinvigorate citizenship.

My third route to universal service is military service. I came of age as the Vietnam War was at its peak, was drafted out of graduate school in late 1968, and spent two years as an enlisted man in the U.S. Marine Corps. The Vietnam-era military draft was widely regarded as arbitrary and unfair, and it was held responsible for dissension within the military as well as the wider society. In the immediate wake of its disaster in Vietnam, the United States made a historic decision to end the draft and institute an All-Volunteer Force (AVF).

Flaws in the All-Volunteer Model

On one level, it's hard to argue with success. The formula of high-quality volunteers, plus intensive training, plus investment in state-of-the-art equipment, has produced the most formidable military in history by far. Evidence suggests that the military's performance, especially since 1990, has bolstered public trust and confidence. For example, a Gallup survey of public opinion trends since the end of the Vietnam War in 1975 indicates that while the share of Americans expressing confidence in religious leaders fell from 68 percent to 45 percent, and for Congress from 40 percent to 29 percent, the percentage expressing confidence in the military rose from under 30 percent to 78 percent. Among 18- to 29-year-olds, the confidence in the military rose from 20 percent to 64 percent. . . .

While these gains in institutional performance and public confidence are impressive, they hardly end the discussion. As every reader of Machiavelli (or the Second Amendment) knows, the organization of the military is embedded in larger issues of citizenship and civic life. It is along these dimensions that the decision to create the AVF has entailed significant costs. First, the AVF reflects and has contributed to the development of what I call *optional citizenship*, the belief that being a citizen involves rights without responsibilities and that we need do for our country only that which we choose. Numerous studies have documented the rise of individual choice as the dominant norm of contemporary American culture, and many young people today believe being a good person—decent, kind, caring, and tolerant—is all it takes to be a good citizen. This duty-free understanding of citizenship is comfortable and undemanding; it is also profoundly mistaken.

Second, the AVF contributes to what I call *spectator citizenship*—the premise that good citizens can simply watch others doing the public's work on their behalf. This outlook makes it possible to decouple the question of whether *we* as a nation should do X from the question of whether *I* would do or participate in X. In a discussion with his students during the Gulf War, Cheyney Ryan, professor of philosophy at the University of Oregon, was struck by "how many of them saw no connection between whether the country should go to war and whether they would . . . be willing to fight in it." A similar disconnection exists today. Far higher percentages of young adults support the war against Iraq than would be willing to serve in it themselves.

Finally, the AVF has widened the gap between the orientation and experience of military personnel and the citizenry as a whole. This is an empirically contested area, but some facts are indisputable. First, since the inauguration of the AVF, the share of officers identifying themselves as Republicans has nearly doubled, from 33 percent to 64 percent. (To be sure, officers were always technically volunteers, but the threat of the draft significantly affected young men's willingness to volunteer for officer candidacy.) Second, and more significantly, the share of elected officials with military experience has declined sharply. From 1900 through 1975, the percentage of members of Congress who were veterans was always higher than in the comparable age cohort of the general population. Since the mid-1990s the congressional percentage has been lower, and it continues to fall.

Lack of military experience does not necessarily imply hostility to the military. Rather, it means ignorance of the nature of military service, as well as diminished capacity and confidence to assess claims that military leaders make. (It is no accident that of all the postwar presidents, Dwight Eisenhower was clearly the most capable of saying no to the military's strategic assessments and requests for additional resources.)

Grounds for Compulsory Service

For all these reasons, I believe we should dramatically expand AmeriCorps, the flagship program of the Corporation for National and Community Service. At the same time, we should reconsider the decision we made 30 years ago to institute an all-volunteer military. I hasten to add that I do not favor reinstituting anything like the Vietnam-era draft. It is hard to see how a reasonable person could prefer that fatally flawed system to today's arrangement. The question, rather, is whether feasible reforms could preserve the gains of the past 30 years while more effectively promoting active, responsible citizenship across the full range of our social, economic, and cultural differences.

Classical liberals will object, of course, on the grounds that it would be an abuse of state power to move toward mandatory universal service. It is worth noting, however, that one of the high priests of classical liberalism disagrees. Consider the opening sentences of Chapter 4 of John Stuart Mill's *On Liberty*, titled "Of the Limits to the Authority of Society Over the Individual":

> [E]veryone who receives the protection of society owes a return for the benefit, and the fact of living in society renders it indispensable that each should be bound to observe a certain line of conduct toward the rest. This conduct consists, first, in not injuring the interests of one another, or rather certain interests which, either by express legal provision or by tacit understanding, ought to be considered as rights; and secondly, in each person's bearing his share (to be fixed on some equitable principle) of the labors and sacrifices incurred for defending the society or its members from injury and molestation. These conditions society is justified in enforcing at all costs to those who endeavor to withhold fulfillment.

It is not difficult to recast Mill's position in the vocabulary of contemporary liberal political thought. Begin with a conception of society as a system of cooperation for mutual advantage. Society is legitimate when the criterion of mutual advantage is broadly satisfied (versus, say, a situation in which the government or some group systematically coerces some for the sake of others). When society meets the standard of broad legitimacy, each citizen has a duty to do his or her fair share to sustain the social arrangements from which all benefit, and society is justified in using its coercive power when necessary to ensure that this duty is performed. That legitimate societal coercion may include mandatory military service in the nation's defense, as well as other required activities that promote broad civic goals.

Brookings scholar Robert Litan has suggested that citizens should be "required to give something to their country in exchange for the full range of rights to which citizenship entitles them." Responding in a quasi-libertarian vein, Bruce Chapman, founder and president of the Seattle-based Discovery Institute, charges that this proposal has "no moral justification." Linking rights to concrete responsibilities, he says, is "contrary to the purposes for which [the United States] was founded and has endured." This simply isn't true. For example, the right to receive GI Bill benefits is linked to the fulfillment of military duties. Even the right to vote (and what could be more central to citizenship than that?) rests on being law-abiding; many states disenfranchise convicted felons during their period of incarceration and probation. As Litan points out, this linkage is hardly tyrannical moralism. Rather, it reflects the bedrock reality that "the rights we enjoy are not free" and that it takes real work—contributions from citizens—to sustain constitutional institutions.

If each individual's ownership of his or her own labor is seen as absolute, then society as such becomes impossible, because no political community can operate without resources, which ultimately must come from *someone*. Public choice theory predicts, and all of human history proves, that no polity of any size can subsist through voluntary contributions alone; the inevitable free riders must be compelled by law, backed by force, to do their part.

The Jury-Duty Analogy

Still, the proponents of a free market/individual choice model might reasonably argue that if a noncoercive approach to military and civilian service can get the job done, there are no valid grounds for legal compulsion. To understand this argument's shortcomings, consider the analogy (or disanalogy) between national service and domestic law enforcement. The latter is divided into two subcategories: voluntary activities (there's no draft for police officers) and mandatory responsibilities (e.g., jury duty). Our current system of national service is all "police" and no "jury." If we conducted domestic law enforcement on that model of service, we'd have what might be called the "All-Volunteer Jury," in which we'd pay enough to ensure that the law enforcement system had a steady flow of jurors.

There are two compelling reasons not to move in this direction. First, citizens who self-select for jury duty would be likely to be unrepresentative of the population as a whole. Those who incur high opportunity costs (the gainfully employed, for example) would tend not to show up. The same considerations that militate against forced exclusion of racial and ethnic groups from jury pools should weigh equally against voluntary self-exclusion based on income or employment status. (We should ask ourselves why these considerations do not apply to the composition of the military.)

Second, all citizens should understand that citizenship is an *office*, not just a *status*. As an office, citizenship confers both rights and duties—indeed, sometimes both simultaneously. Service on juries is simultaneously a right, in the sense that there is a strong presumption against exclusion, and a duty, in the sense that there is a strong presumption against evasion. To move jury duty into the category of voluntary, compensated acts would be to remove one of the last reminders that citizenship is more than a legal status.

Objections to Opt-Out Provisions

I would also offer an argument based on civic self-respect. From the standpoint of military competence, we might do

Universal National Service Would Cure War Fever

A system of universal military service would bring the pain of war to the kitchen tables of America. This may sound harsh, but nothing else could turn a vote for or against war into a vote for or against risking a specific friend or loved one. And personalizing the burdens of war would harness democracy to ensure that any particular war is truly necessary—truly a matter of action being less costly and more moral than inaction.

For this to work, we could not rely on a Vietnam-style draft rife with escape clauses mainly available to the well-off and the well-heeled. It should look more like the draft of World War II, where rich and poor served side by side. It should be flexible enough to accommodate demands such as family and education, perhaps requiring a year or two of service by the time a person reaches the age of 30. As part of a more comprehensive national-service system, there might be nonmilitary options in fields such as medicine, public safety, public education and social services—critical jobs to which nobody could conscientiously object. But placing military service as the cornerstone of this system would transform the decision to go to war from a cost-free intellectual analysis into an appropriately grave choice with intimate personal consequences.

David L. Englin, "Cure for War Fever,"
American Prospect, *October 30, 2002.*

just as well to engage foreigners (the All-Mercenary Armed Forces), as kings and princes did regularly during the 18th century. The cost might well be lower and the military performance just as high. Besides, if we hire foreigners to pick our crops, why shouldn't we hire them to do our fighting?

There is also a moral argument to consider: Even if a mercenary army were reliable and effective, it would be wrong, perhaps shameful, to use our wealth to get noncitizens to fight for us. This is something we should do for ourselves as a self-respecting people. A similar moral principle applies as well in the purely domestic sphere, among citizens.

Consider military recruitment during the Civil War. In April 1861 President Lincoln called for, and quickly received, 75,000 volunteers. But hopes for a quick and easy Union victory were soon dashed, and the first conscription act was passed in March 1863. The act contained two opt-out provisions: An individual facing conscription could pay a $300 fee to avoid a specific draft notice, or he could avoid service altogether by paying a substitute to volunteer for three years.

This law created a complex pattern of individual incentives and unanticipated social outcomes, such as anti-conscription riots among urban workers. Setting these aside, was there anything wrong in principle with these opt-out provisions? I think so. In the first place, there was an obvious distributional unfairness: The well-off could afford to avoid military service, while the poor and the working class couldn't. Historian James McPherson observes that the slogan "a rich man's fight, but a poor man's war" had a powerful impact, particularly among impoverished Irish laborers already chafing against the contempt with which they were regarded by the Protestant elite. Second, even if income and wealth had been more nearly equal, there would have been something wrong in principle with the idea that dollars could purchase exemption from an important civic duty. As McPherson notes, this provision suffered a poor reputation after the Civil War, and the designers of the World War I-era Selective Service Act were careful not to repeat it.

Inequality in the All-Volunteer Force

We can now ask: What is the difference between the use of personal resources to opt *out* of military service and the impact of personal resources (or lack thereof) on the decision to opt *in*? As a practical and a moral matter, the difference is less than the current system's defenders would like to believe. To begin with, the decision to implement the AVF has profoundly affected the military's educational and class composition. During World War II and the Korean War (indeed, through the early 1960s), roughly equal percentages of high school and college graduates served in the military, and about one-third of college graduates were in the enlisted (that is, nonofficer) ranks. Today, enlisted men and women are rarely college graduates, and elite colleges other than the service academies are far less likely to produce military personnel of any rank, officer or enlisted. As a lengthy feature story in the *New York Times* put it, today's military "mirrors a working-class America." Most of the young American men and women dying in Iraq represent working-class families from small-town and rural America.

Many have argued that this income skew is a virtue, not a vice, because the military extends good career opportunities to young men and women whose prospects are otherwise limited. There's something to this argument, of course. But the current system purchases social mobility at the expense of social integration. Today's privileged young people tend to grow up hermetically sealed from the rest of society. Episodic volunteering in soup kitchens doesn't really break the seal. Military service is one of the few experiences that can.

The separation is more than economic. The sons and daughters of the upper-middle classes grow up in a cultural milieu in which certain assumptions tend to be taken for granted. Often, college experiences reinforce rather than challenge these assumptions. Since Vietnam, moreover, many elite colleges and universities have held the military at arm's length, ending ROTC curricula and banning campus-based military recruitment. As a Vietnam-era draftee, I can attest to the role military service plays in expanding mutual awareness across cultural lines. This process is not always pleasant or pretty, but it does pull against the smug incomprehension of the privileged.

In an evocative letter to his sons, Brookings scholar Stephen Hess reflects on his experiences as a draftee and defends military service as a vital socializing experience for children from fortunate families. His argument is instructive:

> Being forced to be the lowest rank . . . , serving for long enough that you can't clearly see "the light at the end of the tunnel," is as close as you will ever come to being a member of society's underclass. To put it bluntly, you will feel in your gut what it means to be at the bottom of the heap. . . . Why should you want to be deprived of your individuality? You shouldn't, of course. But many people are, and you should want to know how this feels, especially if you some day have some responsibility over the lives of other people.

It's a matter not just of compassion, Hess continues, but of respect:

> The middle-class draftee learns to appreciate a lot of talents (and the people who have them) that are not part of the lives you have known, and, after military duty, will know again for the rest of your lives. This will come from being thrown together with—and having to depend on—people who are very different from you and your friends.

A modern democracy, in short, combines a high level of legal equality with an equally high level of economic and social stratification. It is far from inevitable, or even natural, that democratic leaders drawn disproportionately from the upper ranks of society will understand the experiences or respect the contributions of those from the lower ranks. It takes integrative experiences to bring this about. In a society in which economic class largely determines residence and education and in which the fortunate will not willingly associate with the rest, only nonvoluntary institutions cutting across class lines can hope to provide such experiences. If some kind of sustained mandatory service doesn't fill this bill, it is hard to see what will.

AmeriCorps Offers Civilian Options

It is one thing to invoke civic arguments in favor of universal service, quite another to make them real. As we reconsider the all-volunteer recruitment model for armed service, we should also return to Clinton's vision of national service as a package of responsibilities and privileges available to every young American. AmeriCorps has survived repeated efforts to strangle it in the cradle and now enjoys broad bipartisan support. It is time to put our civic money where our civic mouth is—to move steadily from today's quota of 75,000 participants each year to a system in which there's a place for every young American who wants to serve his or her country.

Granted, the financial and administrative burdens of incorporating more than 3 million young people into civilian or military service each year would be prohibitive, at least in the short run. A reasonable goal would be to build over the next decade toward a system that offers 12- to 18-month service opportunities for at least 20 percent of each cohort of physically and mentally eligible 18-year-olds. A random lottery from which only a small percentage are excluded would be (and I believe would be seen as) a fair selection mechanism.

Military manpower requirements would take priority in allocating the service pool thus created. Young people, both in and outside of the pool, could still volunteer for military service, just as they do now. If all slots in the armed forces were filled, the remaining members of that year's service pool would choose among civilian options. If young people did not volunteer in sufficient numbers to satisfy the military's needs, the armed forces would select from among the rest of the pool, for a period of service not to exceed 18 months.

The service pool would function as a floor rather than a ceiling. If 18-year-olds outside the pool wanted to volunteer, they would be guaranteed full-time service opportunities, although they might not have access to their preferred choices.

Creating this program would be neither cheap nor easy. But consider that we have spent decades creating programs that enhance individual self-improvement, consumption, and choice. If we work as hard to foster an ethic of contribution and reciprocity, we can create a richer civic culture that summons, in the words of Lincoln, the better angels of our nature.

| "Universal service never was a good
idea, and it grows worse with time. It
fails militarily, morally, financially, and
politically."

Universal National Service
Is a Bad Idea

Bruce Chapman

*In the following viewpoint, Bruce Chapman objects to universal
national service as unjustified and unworkable. "Service isn't service to the extent that it is compelled," Chapman argues. State
coercion will inevitably breed resentment of and disillusionment
with government in young people, not civic spirit. The military
does not need or want a huge influx of manpower barely out of
high school, he maintains; active-duty expertise requires serious
training and longer-term commitment. Alternatively shunting
someone with scant training into a homeland security post is
"worse than useless"; it would be "dangerous." Domestic charities
can only absorb so many people, he says; thus the government
will end up creating make-work jobs at public expense for unskilled, short-term, reluctant masses, a waste of everyone's time
and money. Bruce Chapman is founder and president of the Dis-*

Bruce Chapman, "A Bad Idea Whose Time Is Past: The Case Against Universal Service," *Brookings Review*, vol. 20, Fall 2002, pp. 10–13. Copyright 2002 Brookings Institution. Reproduced by permission.

covery Institute, a Seattle-based conservative think tank and educational foundation best known for its support of intelligent design creationism and skepticism of Darwinian evolution. His 1967 book The Wrong Man in Uniform *made an early case for an all-volunteer military.*

As you read, consider the following questions:

1. How does Chapman counter the argument that universal national service is, like jury duty, an obligation to one's country in exchange for the rights of citizenship?
2. What does Chapman estimate would be the total cost to the federal government for each "involuntary volunteer" in a universal national service program modeled after AmeriCorps?
3. What alternatives to universal national service would inspire American youth to serve their country, according to the author?

If each woman in China could only be persuaded to lower the hem of her skirt one inch, some 19th-century English merchants reasoned, the looms of Manchester could spin forever. Like that romantic calculation, the idea of universal service assumes a mythical economic and cultural system where people behave as you would like them to, with motivations of which you approve. Unlike it, universal service adds coercion to ensure compliance.

Universal service never was a good idea, and it grows worse with time. It fails militarily, morally, financially, and politically.

For almost a century, universal service has brought forth new advocates, each desiring to enlist all youth in something. Only the justifications keep changing. Today's justification is "homeland security." But is it realistic to suggest that youth who help guard a "public or private facility" (let alone those who stuff envelopes at some charity's office) are "shouldering the burden of war" in the same way as a soldier in Afghanistan?

I don't want to attach to Robert Litan [an advocate of universal service] all the customary arguments that universal service advocates have been promoting for years, especially because he states that "advocating universal service before September 11 would have been unthinkable" (at least to him). Except in times of mass conflict, such as the Civil War and the two World Wars, there has never been much of a reason for universal service. Still, the varied arguments for it need to be addressed.

No Military Case

Universal service is not needed on military grounds. We eliminated the draft three decades ago in part because the armed services found that they needed relatively fewer recruits to serve longer than conscription provided. As the numbers that were needed shrank, the unfairness of the draft became ever more apparent—and offensive. Youth, ever ingenious, found ways to get deferments, decamp to Canada, make themselves a nuisance to everyone in authority—and make those who did serve feel like chumps. Many of the young people who objected to military service availed themselves of alternative service, but no one seriously believed that most "conscientious objectors" were "shouldering the burden of war" in a way comparable to those fighting in the field.

The government took advantage of its free supply of almost unlimited manpower by underpaying its servicemen, thereby losing many recruits who might have chosen a military career. Raising the pay when the volunteer force was introduced changed the incentives and—surprise—eliminated the need for the draft. The all-volunteer force has been a big success.

Leaders in today's [2002's] increasingly sophisticated, highly trained military now are talking of further manpower cuts. They have no interest in short-term soldiers of any kind and give no support to a return to conscription. The idea of using universal service to round up young men and women who, instead of direct military service, could be counted on to guard a "public or private facility," as [Brookings Institution economist Robert] Litan proposes is naive. In Litan's plan, youth would be obligated for only a year—slightly less, if AmeriCorps were the model. [AmeriCorps, founded by the National and Community Service Act of 1993, is the central organizer of U.S. local, state, and national service programs such as VISTA and the National Civilian Community Corps. Members work for 10 to 12 months and receive education benefits.] Philip Gold, a [former] colleague at Discovery Institute and author of the post–September 11 book *Against All Terrors: This Nation's Next Defense*, points out that "if the object is fighting, a person trained only for a few months is useless. In a noncombat defense position, he would be worse than useless. He would be dangerous."

Litan's interest in compulsory service grew partly out of recent work on Israel. According to Gold, armed guards in Israel do protect day care centers, for example. But all have had serious military training and two to three years of active duty, followed by service in the active reserves. A population with widespread military training and service can accomplish things that a civilian volunteer program cannot.

Litan anticipates nothing comparable from short-term universal servicemen and -women. A one-year obligation, under the AmeriCorps example, works out to only 1,700 hours— roughly 10 months of 40-hour weeks. By the time the compulsory volunteers were trained, it would be time for them to muster out. The system would be roiled by constant turnover. It is surely unrealistic to expect to fill security jobs with youths who will be around for only a few months. Ask yourself, would you rather have a paid and trained person or a conscripted teenager inspecting the seaport for possible terrorists?

No Moral Justification

Trying to justify universal service on moral grounds is also a mistake, and a serious one. Morally, service isn't service to the extent it is compelled. Involuntary voluntarism is like hot snow. And allowing the pay to approach (let alone surpass) that available to ordinary workers of the same age performing the same tasks as the stipended and officially applauded "volunteers" stigmatizes the private sector. (The military recruit of today is sometimes called a volunteer only because he is not conscripted. His service is more commendable morally than that of some other paid employee because he is prepared to risk his life.)

Universal service advocates such as Litan are on especially shaky ground when charging that citizens should be "required to give something to their country in exchange for the full range of rights to which citizenship entitles them." This cuts against the grain of U.S. history and traditions. Citizens here are expected to be law-abiding, and they are called to jury duty—and to the military if absolutely necessary. They are encouraged (not forced) to vote and to render voluntary service—which Americans famously do. But to require such service before the rights of citizenship are extended is simply contrary to the purposes for which the country was founded and has endured. The Founders had a keen awareness of the ways that the state could tyrannize the people, and taking the people's liberty away to serve some specious government purpose unattached to national survival is a project that would horrify them.

I also raise this practical question: exactly which citizenship rights will Litan deny those people who decline to perform government-approved national service? What will be done to punish the activist who thinks he can do more to serve humanity through a political party than through pre-scribed government service? Or the young religious mission-ary who would rather save souls than guard a pier for a few months? How about—at the other end of the virtue spec-trum—the young drug dealer who is only too happy to help guard the pier? Will you keep him out of the service of his choice and compel him to do rehab as his form of "service"?

Outside of mass mobilization for war—or in the special case of Israel, a small nation effectively on constant alert—the only modern nations that have conscripted labor to meet as-sorted, centrally decreed social purposes have been totalitarian regimes. In those lands, the object, as much as anything, has been to indoctrinate youth in the morality of the state. Litan may not have such goals in mind, but many universal service advocates want to use conscription to straighten out the next generation—to their approved standards. No doubt many—most?—think they can inculcate a sense of voluntary service through compulsory service.

In reality, however, no previous generation of youth has been so encouraged to volunteer for various approved, state-sponsored social causes. In many high schools in the United States, students cannot get a diploma without performing a certain number of hours of approved "community service." Does a child who must perform service to graduate from high school develop a high sense of what it means to help others? Does a student who learns that almost anything counts to-ward the service requirement—so long as he doesn't get paid—develop a keen sense of civil calling? Or does he hone his skill at gaming the system? And why, if we have this ser-vice requirement in high school—and some colleges—do we need yet another one for the year after high school?

Unintended Consequences

Universal service (indeed any national service scheme that achieves demographic heft) is a case study in unintended con-

Mandatory Service Is Cost Prohibitive

Some Americans say national service should be required of everyone; others believe service should never be coerced.

This fundamental split is not new. Americans have always been divided on the question of whether some form of national service should be mandatory. In part, the dichotomy stems from two seemingly contradictory strains in the American character: a deep belief in helping others—specially the less fortunate—and an equally strong sense of self-reliance. . . .

Some government officials oppose mandatory service because they say the cost of setting up and operating a nationwide national service program would be prohibitive. When the White House announced it was eliminating the NCCC's [National Civilian Community Corps] funding, Tom Schatz, president of Citizens Against Government Waste, told Fox News, "We thought AmeriCorps was always expensive. I give the administration credit for evaluating a program and proposing its elimination."

Likewise, James Bovard, president and founder of the Competitive Enterprise Institute, said, "It's always been a boondoggle [waste of time and money], and it will always be a boondoggle when you are rounding up people and paying them for doing good deeds."

John Greenya, "National Service,"
CQ Researcher, June 30, 2006.

sequences. One surprise for liberals might be a growing disillusionment with the government and the way it wastes money. Today's youth trust the government and are immensely patriotic, but bureaucratized service requirements could cure that. Another unintended consequence might be instruction in how government make-work is a tax on one's freedom and an irritating distraction from education goals and serious career development. Conservatives of a sardonic nature might come to appreciate the prospect of generations growing to adulthood with firsthand experience of government's impertinence. It would not be necessary thereafter to exhort the veterans of such unnecessary compulsion to resist the claims of government over the rest of their lives.

Universal service likewise would be an invitation to scandal. The military draft was bad enough, dispatching the budding scientist to pick up paper on a base's roadsides and sending the sickly malcontent to deliver meal trays to patients in base hospitals. People with powerful parents got cushy positions, while the poor got the onerous tasks. When labor is both free and abundant, it will be squandered and abused. If that was true in eras when mass armies were raised, what can one expect in a time when only a small fraction of the population is needed to operate our high-tech military?

No Financial Justification

The cost of universal service would be prohibitive. Direct costs would include those for assembling, sorting (and sorting out), allocating, and training several million youth in an unending manpower convoy. Indirect costs include clothing and providing initial medical attention, insurance, the law enforcement associated with such large numbers (no small expense in the army, even with presumably higher discipline), housing, and the periodic "leave" arrangements.

The $20,000 per involuntary volunteer estimated by Litan is too low. The more realistic total figure would be more like $27,000 to $30,000. First, the federal cost for a full-time AmeriCorps member is about $16,000, according to AmeriCorps officials. And that, recall, is for an average 10-month stint, so add another $3,000 or so for a 12-month term of service. (The $10,000 figure cited by Litan appears to average the cost of part-time volunteers with that of full-time volunteers.)

Giving the involuntary volunteers the AmeriCorps education benefit of some $4,000 brings the total to about $23,000 of federal contribution for the full-time, one-year participant, which, with local or private match, will easily reach a total cost of some $30,000. Few unskilled young people just out of school make that in private employment!

Because organized compulsion costs more than real volunteering, however, the indirect expenses for governments would be still greater. Chief among these are the hidden financial costs of universal national service to the economy in the form of forgone labor. That problem plagued the old draft and would be more acute now. The United States has suffered a labor shortage for most of the past two decades, with the dearth of educated and trained labor especially serious. Yet universal service advocates want to pluck out of the employment ranks some 4 million people a year and apply a command-and-control approach to their optimal use. How can we even calculate the waste?

Litan says that in 1995 the GAO [Government Accountability Office] "positively evaluated" a cost-benefit study of three AmeriCorps programs that found them to produce quantifiable monetary benefits of $1.68 to $2.58 for every dollar invested. But Litan overstates the GAO's "positive evaluation" of the private study's findings. The GAO study merely analyzes the methodology of the private study based on the assumptions that are baked into it. These assumptions (of future benefits and their dollar values) are inherently "problematic," based as they are on "projected data." And neither the GAO nor the private study whose methodology it checked says anything about the applicability of the private study to some universal service program. Inferring GAO endorsement for some putative financial benefits from a national service scheme—let alone a program of compulsory national service—is not good economics.

By contrast, a review of the literature and evidence of government spending by William Niskanen, former chairman of the President's Council of Economic Advisors (under Ronald Reagan), concluded that "the marginal cost of government spending and taxes in the United States may be about $2.75 per additional dollar of tax revenue." As the late Nobel economist Frederick Hayek said, "There is only one problem with socialism. It does not work."

The cost of universal service for one year would not be $80 billion, with certain additional economic benefits, as Litan would have it, but roughly $120 billion, with considerable additional losses to the economy as a whole.

No Practical or Political Worth

There is no demand for all these volunteers, as charities themselves have pointed out. Nonprofits can absorb only so many unseasoned, unskilled, short-term "volunteers," particularly when some of the "volunteers" are reluctant, to say the least. So what is the point? Is it political?

Some universal service advocates (not Litan) have cited a January 2002 survey by Lake Snell Perry & Associates, The Tarrance Group, Inc. (The survey was conducted for the Center for Information and Research in Civic Learning & Engagement, the Center for Democracy & Citizenship, and The Partnership for Trust in Government at the Council for Excellence in Government.) The study shows strong support among youth for universal service. But these advocates usually neglect to mention that this support is based on a stated assumption in the survey question that such service would be "an alternative to (compulsory) military service should one be instituted." A truer reflection of youthful opinion is found in the survey's largely unreported question on community service as a requirement for high school graduation. That program is overwhelmingly opposed—by a 35 percent margin among current high school students. Interestingly, the same survey shows that "instituting civics and government course requirements in schools is favored by a 15-point margin by current high school students."

This should tell us something. Putting $120 billion, or even $80 billion, into a universal national service scheme would be a waste. But how about spending some tiny corner of that money on teaching kids about real—that is, voluntary—service? How about paying to teach students about representative democracy and their part in it as voters and volunteers or about the way our economy works and how to prepare for successful participation in it? Or to teach them American history (for many, it would be a new course) in a way that inspired them with the stories of men and women, great and humble, who have rendered notable service in their communities, nation, and world.

The way to get a nation of volunteers is to showcase voluntary service, praise it, reward it, and revere it. The way to sabotage voluntary service is to coerce it, bureaucratize it, nationalize it, cloak it in political correctness, and pay for it to the point where the "volunteer" makes out better than the poor soul of the same age who works for a living. Voluntary service blesses the one who serves as well as those to whom he renders service. Universal service would be civic virtue perverted into a civic vice.

"The way to increase the proportion of highly educated and relatively well-to-do Americans in our armed forces is to institute Junior ROTC programs in every high school in the country."

Revive the ROTC Program to Expand the All-Volunteer Armed Forces

Stanley Kurtz

Stanley Kurtz is a contributing editor at the National Review *and a senior fellow at the Ethics and Public Policy Center, a Washington, D.C., institute that examines public policy issues within the Judeo-Christian moral tradition. In the following viewpoint, Kurtz argues that antimilitary cultural attitudes beginning in the 1960s are behind the disappearance of the Reserve Officer Training Corps (ROTC) military preparatory programs once widespread in high schools and on college campuses. Kurtz urges the reinstatement of ROTC instead of universal national service or the military draft to reestablish respect for military service; attract bright, relatively well-to-do enlistees; and inculcate in all Americans positive values such as discipline, shared sacrifice, and national pride.*

As you read, consider the following questions:

1. What objections does Kurtz raise to Congressman Charles Rangel's proposal to establish universal national service?

2. How did the enlistment of Frank Schaeffer's son, described by the author, force Schaeffer to reassess his own prejudices against the armed forces?

3. What new proposal to augment U.S. military forces does Kurtz approve of in addition to revitalizing the ROTC movement?

Congressman Charles Rangel has introduced a measure to require all U.S. citizens or permanent residents aged 18 to 26 to complete two years of compulsory service, inside or outside the military. His stated reasons for this are to ensure shared sacrifice among all Americans in the event of a war, and to induce caution in legislators who would know that, in voting for war, their own children might be placed in harm's way.

Yet Congressman Rangel's proposal goes far beyond that, chiefly because it would create a gigantic government make-work program for the millions of drafted Americans who would not serve in the military (not to mention the cost of feeding, housing, and managing a huge section of the population). While I do see advantages in inculcating an ethic of service, ultimately I think the problems of a huge, mandatory, government run sector of the economy outweigh any benefits.

Put ROTC Back on Campuses

On the other hand, there is a more-efficient way to meet Congressman Rangel's legitimate concerns. The way to increase the proportion of highly educated and relatively well-to-do Americans in our armed forces is to institute Junior ROTC programs in every high school in the country. We should also return the ROTC to America's most-prestigious college campuses.

Leading Universities Should Lead ROTC's Comeback

[On May 28, 2007], Harvard University will mark its 36th consecutive Memorial Day without the Reserve Officer Training Corps. The story is similar at many other of the nation's finest schools. Cowed university administrators kicked ROTC off campus in an anti-Vietnam fervor and never looked back, not seriously. Years turned into decades and the arguments changed, but the policies did not. It's time for Harvard, Columbia, Yale and other schools to heed what President Bush said [in May 2007]: "It should not be hard for our great schools of learning to find room to honor the service of men and women who are standing up to defend the freedoms that make the work of our universities possible." It's time to give ROTC a chance.

W.F. Buckley, "Bring Back ROTC,"
Power Line Forum, May 27, 2007.

The real barrier to the participation of educated, upper-middle-class recruits in our armed forces is cultural. The root of the problem is the deep hostility to our military inculcated by the antiwar movement of the sixties—a hostility now institutionalized at our finest colleges and universities. If we could overcome that cultural barrier, then the sacrifice (and honor) of military service would be more equally shared by all sectors of our country. That, in turn, would mean that legislators would be far more likely to know someone in military service. This, by the way, is not an idea that I have developed for the purpose of countering Congressman Rangel's legislation. It is something I have already proposed.

The model for the attitude toward the military that we should be seeking is the popular new book, *Keeping Faith: A Father Son Journey About Love and the United States Marine*

Corps. Keeping Faith is the story of Frank Schaeffer, a "Volvo driving, higher education worshiping" novelist, with two children who graduated from top universities. When Frank's youngest son, John, joined the Marine Corps straight out of high school, this father was forced to recognize and overcome his own prejudice—and the prejudice of his friends and neighbors—against our military. The story of Frank Schaeffer's newfound pride in his Marine son—and of his struggle against the anti-military biases of his upper-middle-class friends—is the real solution to the problems raised by Congressman Rangel.

So legislators who understand the drawbacks of a compulsory national-service program, but who want to meet Congressman Rangel's legitimate concerns, can now support wide dissemination of JROTC programs to American high schools, and enforcement of the Solomon amendment, which would return ROTC to our college campuses.

Shorten Enlistment Options

Another way of augmenting our forces, increasing their quality, and taking recruits from a broader swath of society was adopted [in 2003]. President Bush signed into law a new, short-term "citizen soldier" enlistment track, a proposal sponsored by Senators Evan Bayh and John McCain. A shorter term of service will draw volunteers committed to careers in the private sector. (And some of these, no doubt, will change their mind and turn toward a military career once enlisted.) Marc Magee and Steven Nider, of the Progressive Policy Institute (the think tank affiliated with the centrist Democratic Leadership Council), have laid out the rationale for the citizen-soldier enlistment track. You can also read about the proposal here.

Once the new citizen-soldier initiative is combined with public support for an expanded JROTC and ROTC, it will be that much easier to do what I think we need to do—expand our all-volunteer forces back up to something approaching Gulf War levels. North Korea may already have called our bluff because it understood that our forces were too small to handle Iraq and a Korean crisis at the same time. And an extended occupation of Iraq will stretch our forces still further. With nuclear proliferation likely to precipitate periodic crises for the foreseeable future, we need a larger military. With luck, we will be able to achieve that on a voluntary basis. But to do so, we'll need to broaden the pool of quality recruits. A national commitment to ROTC and JROTC is the way to do that. And the new citizen-soldier enlistment track will surely help as well.

As I have said on numerous occasions, we cannot and should not exclude the possibility of reviving the draft. I don't think we've begun to see the end of the military problems facing this nation in an era of terrorism and nuclear proliferation. But before we resort to a draft (at which point, a lottery would make more sense than universal national service), we should try to expand our all-volunteer forces. By doing so with the help of a revitalized ROTC and JROTC program, we can insure that Congressman Rangel's concerns about shared sacrifice are met.

"The idea of signing up foreigners who are seeking US citizenship is gaining traction as a way to address a critical need for the Pentagon."

Recruitment of Foreigners Would Boost Military Ranks

Bryan Bender

The idea of hiring foreigners to fight U.S. wars is a radical and highly charged issue, journalist Bryan Bender writes in the following viewpoint, but it is getting serious consideration as the war in Iraq stretches military manpower. At present, only immigrants legally residing in the United States are eligible to enlist, but recently amended U.S. law gives the Pentagon the authority to bring immigrants into the country, and the armed forces, in the interest of national security. There are historical precedents for such a practice, Bender argues: German and French soldiers served alongside colonists in the American Revolution, Nepalese soldiers serve in the British army, and the Swiss Guard and French Foreign Legion have always been multinational forces. If joining the army means a fast track to citizenship, Bender concludes, many would line up and the military draft would be unnecessary to sustain the all-volunteer force. Bryan Bender is a staff writer for the The Boston Globe.

As you read, consider the following questions:

1. How many noncitizens currently serve in the U.S. armed forces, according to Bender?

2. Why does the Hispanic rights advocacy group National Council of La Raza oppose the enlistment of foreign nationals, according to the author?

3. What percentage of Union soldiers in the Civil War were immigrants, according to Max Boot, as quoted by the author?

The armed forces, already struggling to meet recruiting goals, are considering expanding the number of noncitizens in the ranks—including disputed proposals to open recruiting stations overseas and putting more immigrants on a faster track to U.S. citizenship if they volunteer—according to Pentagon officials.

Foreign citizens serving in the U.S. military is a highly charged issue, which could expose the Pentagon to criticism that it is essentially using mercenaries to defend the country. Other analysts voice concern that a large contingent of noncitizens under arms could jeopardize national security or reflect badly on Americans' willingness to serve in uniform.

The idea of signing up foreigners who are seeking U.S. citizenship is gaining traction as a way to address a critical need for the Pentagon, while fully absorbing some of the roughly one million immigrants that enter the United States legally each year.

Accelerate Citizenship for Legal-Resident Volunteers

The proposal to induct more noncitizens which is still largely on the drawing board, has to clear a number or hurdles. So far, the Pentagon has been quiet about specifics—including who would be eligible to join, where the recruiting stations would be, and what the minimum standards might involve, including English proficiency. In the meantime, the Pentagon and immigration authorities have expanded a program that accelerates citizenship for legal residents who volunteer for the military.

And since Sept. 11, 2001, the number of immigrants in uniform who have become U.S. citizens has increased from 750 in 2001 to almost 4,600 [in 2005], according to military statistics.

With severe manpower strains because of the wars in Iraq and Afghanistan—and a mandate to expand the overall size of the military—the Pentagon is under pressure to consider a variety of proposals revolving foreign recruits, according to a military affairs analyst.

"It works as a military idea and it works in the context of American immigration," said Thomas Donnelly, a military scholar at the conservative American Enterprise Institute in Washington and a leading proponent of recruiting more foreigners to serve in the military.

As the wars in Iraq and Afghanistan grind on, the Pentagon has warned Congress and the White House that the military is stretched "to the breaking point."

Both President Bush and Robert M. Gates, his defense secretary, have acknowledged that the total size of the military must be expanded to help alleviate the strain on ground troops, many of whom have been deployed repeatedly in combat theaters.

Bush said [in December 2006] that he has ordered Gates to come up with a plan for the first significant increase in ground forces since the end of the Cold War. Democrats who are preparing to take control of Congress, meanwhile, promise to make increasing the size of the military one of their top legislative priorities in 2007.

"With today's demands [as of December 2006] placing such a high strain on our service members, it becomes more crucial than ever that we work to alleviate their burden," said

Representative Ike Skelton, a Missouri Democrat who is set to chair the House Armed Services Committee, and who has been calling for a larger Army for more than a decade.

But it would take years and billions of dollars to recruit, train, and equip the 30,000 troops and 5,000 Marines the Pentagon says it needs. And military recruiters, fighting the perception that signing up means a ticket to Baghdad, have had to rely on financial incentives and lower standards to meet their quotas.

That has led Pentagon officials to consider casting a wider net for noncitizens who are already here, said Lieutenant Colonel Bryan Hilferty, an Army spokesman.

Already, the Army and the Immigration and Customs Enforcement division of the Department of Homeland Security have "made it easier for green-card holders who do enlist to get their citizenship," Hilferty said.

Bring In Foreign Nationals

Other Army Officials, who asked not to be identified, said personnel officials are working with Congress and other parts of the government to test the feasibility of going beyond U.S. borders to recruit soldiers and Marines.

Currently, Pentagon policy stipulates that only immigrants legally residing in the United States are eligible to enlist. There are currently about 30,000 noncitizens who serve in the U.S. armed forces, making up about 2 percent of the active-duty force, according to statistics from the military and the Council on Foreign Relations. About 100 noncitizens have died in Iraq and Afghanistan.

A recent change in U.S. law, however, gave the Pentagon authority to bring immigrants to the United States if it determines it is vital to national security. So far, the Pentagon has not taken advantage of it, but the calls are growing to take use the new authority.

The Push to Recruit Undocumented Aliens

If the Pentagon were to decide to exercise its new prerogative [per the National Defense Authorization Act of 2006] and begin to recruit undocumented youth in order to grow the Army and Marines, the most obvious selling point would be permanent residency and eventual citizenship. This is one of the little-known aspects of the DREAM Act, legislation that would grant conditional residency to most undocumented high school graduates and permanent residency in exchange for the successful completion of two years of college or two years of military service. . . .

The expansion of the recruiting pool to include the undocumented would be a recruiting command's dream and may be the only way for the Pentagon to increase the size of the Army and Marine Corps. A 2006 study by the Migration Policy Institute calculated that passage of the DREAM Act "would *immediately* make 360,000 unauthorized high school graduates aged 18 to 24 eligible for conditional legal status [and] that about 715,000 unauthorized youth between ages 5 and 17 would become eligible. . .sometime in the future."

Jorge Mariscal, "Growing the Military: Who Will Serve?"
Draft NOtices, *Committee Opposed to Militarism and the Draft,*
January–March 2007.

Indeed, some top military thinkers believe the United States should go as far as targeting foreigners in their native countries.

"It's a little dramatic," said Michael O'Hanlon, a military specialist at the nonpartisan Brookings Institution and another supporter of the proposal. "But if you don't get some new idea how to do this, we will not be able to achieve an increase" in the size of the armed forces.

"We have already done the standard things to recruit new soldiers, including using more recruiters and new advertising campaigns," O'Hanlon added.

O'Hanlon and others noted that the country has relied before on sizable numbers of noncitizens to serve in the military—in the Revolutionary War, for example, German and French soldiers served alongside the colonists, and locals were recruited into U.S. ranks to fight insurgents in the Philippines.

Other nations have recruited foreign citizens: In France, the famed Foreign Legion relies on about 8,000 noncitizens; Nepalese soldiers called Gurkhas have fought and died with British Army forces for two centuries; and the Swiss Guard, which protects the Vatican, consists of troops who hail from many nations.

"It is not without historical precedent," said Donnelly, author of a recent book titled *The Army We Need*, which advocates a larger military.

Still, to some military officials and civil rights groups, relying on large number of foreigners to serve in the military is offensive.

Overcoming Resistance Is Difficult

The Hispanic rights advocacy group National Council of La Raza has said the plan sends the wrong message that Americans themselves are not willing to sacrifice to defend their country. Officials have also raised concerns that immigrants would be disproportionately sent to the front lines as "cannon fodder" in any conflict.

Some within the Army privately express concern that a big push to recruit noncitizens would smack of "the decline of the American empire," as one Army official who asked not to be identified put it.

Officially, the military remains confident that it can meet recruiting goals—no matter how large the military is increased—without having to rely on foreigners.

"The Army can grow to whatever size the nation wants us to grow to," Hilferty said. "National defense is a national challenge, not the Army's challenge."

He pointed out that just 15 years ago, during the Gulf War, the Army had a total of about 730,000 active-duty soldiers, amounting to about one American in 350 who were serving in the active-duty Army.

"Today, with 300 million Americans and about 500,000 active-duty soldiers, only about one American in 600 is an active-duty soldier," he said. "America did then, and we do now, have an all-volunteer force, and I see no reason why America couldn't increase the number of Americans serving."

But Max Boot, a national security specialist at the Council on Foreign Relations, said that the number of noncitizens the armed forces have now is relatively small by historical standards.

"In the 19th century, when the foreign-born population of the United States was much higher, so was the percentage of foreigners serving in the military," Boot wrote in 2005.

"During the Civil War, at least 20 percent of Union soldiers were immigrants, and many of them had just stepped off the boat before donning a blue uniform. There were even entire units, like the 15th Wisconsin Volunteer Infantry [the Scandinavian Regiment] and General Louis Blenker's German Division, where English was hardly spoken."

"The military would do well today to open its ranks not only to legal immigrants but also to illegal ones and, as important, to untold numbers of young men and women who are not here now but would like to come," Boot added.

"No doubt many would be willing to serve for some set period, in return for one of the world's most precious commodities—US citizenship. Some might deride those who sign up as mercenaries, but these troops would have significantly different motives than the usual soldier of fortune."

> *"With a growing military presence around the world, recruitment difficulties, and public policy determined by war profiteers, the U.S. has become the largest consumer of [the privatized military industry] of any nation."*

The U.S. Military Can Hire Private Contractors

Michelle Gutiérrez

In the following viewpoint, writer Michelle Gutiérrez describes the growth of the privatized military industry (PMI). The U.S. military hires private contractors for security functions, which means the contractors carry arms, as well as for many noncombat jobs at the U.S./Mexico border and in Latin America in the war against drugs and in Iraq, where private contractors make up 15 percent of the total U.S. troop strength. Employing mercenaries is a controversial strategy for two reasons, Gutiérrez argues. First, private contractors are neither bound by local laws nor considered soldiers and so face no sanctions for brutal behavior that the regular army cannot employ. Second, many private contractors are poor workers from developing countries who

Michelle Gutiérrez, "Private Soldiers and the New Age of Warfare," *Draft NOtices*, Committee Opposed to Militarism and the Draft, January–March 2006. Reproduced by permission.

are exploited by labor brokers and may not have deliberately put themselves in harm's way. Nevertheless, the use of PMI gives the Pentagon a way to expand the military without reinstating a military draft.

As you read, consider the following questions:

1. How many private contractors are serving in Iraq, in the author's 2006 estimate?
2. Where do private military contractors get their training, according to Gutiérrez?
3. How were private contractors implicated in the Abu Ghraib prisoner abuse scandal in Iraq, according to the author?

After the collapse of the Berlin Wall when militaries seemingly shrank in size, many military personnel from around the globe became part of the privatized military industry (PMI). PMI has grown to operate in more than 50 nations, generating over $100 billion in revenue annually. With a growing military presence around the world, recruitment difficulties, and public policy determined by war profiteers, the U.S. has become the largest consumer of PMI of any nation. While the official number of private contractors in Iraq has been recorded at 20,000, which represents 15% of the troop strength, this figure only accounts for security contractors, those who "carry arms." Recent estimates of all private contractors have been as high as 100,000. Clearly, private contractors are essential for operations in Iraq, and U.S. military projects are fueling this growing business.

The Fast-Growing Privatized Military Industry

Since the mid 1990s, PMI has been one of the fastest growing industries. Military downsizing, smaller scale conflicts, and the ideological push toward privatization have contributed to the

The Military's Dependence on Private Contractors

So far, over one million U.S. military personnel have served in Iraq and Afghanistan, with some 341,000 already doing the dreaded double-deployments (and many now entering triple-deployment territory). The military has moved troops into Iraq from all over the world, including previously untouchable Cold War detachments in Korea, Germany, and Alaska, and it's still "scrambling" to keep 17 battalions regularly in Iraq, many severely undermanned. These shortages have led to an increasing dependence on expensive private security contractors, who themselves add to the Pentagon's recruitment problems by hiring away otherwise re-upable military personnel for four times the wages paid in the Army.

Michael Schwartz, "Letting in the Draft,"
Alternet.org, April 30, 2005.

industry's growth. The U.S. has used private contractors in the small "peace-keeping" conflicts at the U.S.-Mexico border, to train militaries in Latin America for the "war against drugs," and for an array of duties in Iraq, including transportation, security, construction, food service, housing, laundry, and other non-combat jobs that support military operations.

Contractors for these security and other essential services come from various countries around the world. Many security officials now working in Iraq were once trained by the United States. Another source is elite security personnel who previously worked under such notables as the brutal dictator Augusto Pinochet in Chile, the war criminal Slobodan Milosevic in Yugoslavia, and military officials in El Salvador. Former apartheid special forces from South Africa make up the largest number of armed security personnel in Iraq. In fact, Aegis

Defense Systems, originally formed in the 1980s as Executive Outcomes by South African military elites, won a $1.8 billion contract to coordinate all other private security companies in Iraq.

Sometimes trained by the U.S. in repressive war tactics, private contractors allow the government to circumvent international law that protects civilians and enemies during war. For example, in Iraq confusion arises because private contractors are neither bound by local laws nor are they technically considered soldiers. In another case in 1998, while under contract to the U.S. military to spray toxic herbicide over fields in Bosnia (without regard to the devastating consequences on the villagers below), personnel of the U.S.-based DynCorp were caught trafficking sex slaves, but no charges were made. The advantage to the government, and the problem for everyone else, is that private firms remain unaccountable to anyone, even for the most egregious behavior. In Abu Ghraib, for example, PMIs were contracted to translate for interrogators but were later implicated in abuse, torture, execution, and rape of prisoners without facing sanctions.

Risks of Contract Service Are High

Another little-known aspect of PMI is the use of contractors from developing countries. While some individuals can make up to $1,000 a day working for a military firm, other contracted workers make much less. Coming primarily from Nepal, the Philippines, and Bangladesh, but also from Latin America, these private contractors are paid low wages and work in the most dangerous conditions, usually performing grunt work such as cooking, serving, and cleaning. While it may appear that workers from the poorest nations put themselves in harm's way only because they are in need of money, there have been widespread reports that many of these people are intentionally misled and abused by labor brokers, who find the jobs and move laborers from base to base. Often workers are promised a non-dangerous zone to work. They take loans to pay for their travel, but in many cases their brokers then inform them that their assignments have changed and they end up in Iraq. Because they owe money, many are trapped there, becoming modern-day indentured servants.

The danger to these low-paid contracted workers is clear. Individuals doing menial labor account for one-third of the 255 contractors reported killed in Iraq since March 2003. There is little protection of these workers' rights. The dangerous conditions have caused the governments in the Philippines and Nepal to forbid their citizens to work in Iraq, but labor brokers still get contracts through loopholes. For example, the *Los Angeles Times* reported that even after their government's disapproval, there are more than 5,000 Nepalese working in Iraq.

PMI has been used by the United States since the war in Vietnam. However, its exponential growth in recent years must bring us to ask questions about the ways in which wars are being fought. Few Americans realize that the war in Iraq would not be possible without the labor of people from the Philippines, Chile, or Nepal. The "coalition forces" could not sustain the U.S. occupation without these contractors. The use of PMI demonstrates clearly that markets are more important than workers' rights or democratic accountability for yet another U.S. neocolonial project.

> *"Virtually all defense analysts (in or out of uniform) concur that expanding the ground forces will not alleviate the current pressure on U.S. troops."*

The United States Should Not Pursue Military Expansion

Gordon Adams

The problem of finding ways to expand the all-volunteer army without reinstating the military draft is based on a false premise—that is, America needs more troops—Gordon Adams argues in the following viewpoint. Adams contends that the army is stressed and stretched too thin not because it has too few soldiers but because the United States is pursuing a flawed foreign policy and should neither be fighting a war in Iraq nor playing "global cop" and deploying forces to trouble spots all over the world. The United States cannot shore up failed regimes, successfully wage counterinsurgency campaigns, or unilaterally sustain foreign occupations where it is not welcome, he maintains. Neither can it defeat terrorism with a larger army; doing so will take skilled special forces, allied cooperation, diplomacy, and tracking international flows of money, none of which is the military's job. Adams concludes that the best course is to with

Gordon Adams, "The Problem with Expanding the U.S. Military," *Bulletin of the Atomic Scientists*, May 1, 2007. Copyright © 2007 *Bulletin of the Atomic Scientists*. Reproduced by permission of *Bulletin of the Atomic Scientists: The Magazine of Global Security News & Analysis*.

draw and rebuild American military forces (and its international reputation and leadership) with a different political strategy. Gordon Adams teaches international affairs and national security at the Elliott School of International Affairs at George Washington University in Washington, D.C.

As you read, consider the following questions:

1. Why will expanding ground forces not alleviate the current pressure on U.S. troops in Iraq, according to Adams?
2. Why is expanding ground forces a bad strategy in dealing with conflict in Pakistan, Indonesia, North Korea, or Iran, in the author's opinion?
3. What does Adams say is the problem with appropriating the necessary $112 billion to raise the additional forces called for by President George W. Bush in 2007?

The United States is at war; well, its military is anyway. The United States chose this war, chose badly, and conducted it even more poorly. Washington amply demonstrated that it's not capable of exporting democracy and reconstructing a country—especially when that country is in the midst of a civil war unleashed by U.S. incompetence. Perhaps we're learning that the world is a vastly more complicated place than our naive assumptions led us to believe. Sadly, some in the United States think that enlarging the military will fix our failures in this war and enable us to conduct a similar intervention with more success in the future.

Expanding the Military Won't Help the Situation in Iraq

These people should take a look at the global reality: The United States hasn't been this safe since the start of the Cold War; it's without military peer; and it no longer needs to worry about being obliterated by a massive nuclear strike.

And yet, it is said, the United States needs more soldiers because the world is a dangerous place. As Frederick Kagan and Michael O'Hanlon wrote in a recent Stanley Foundation brief ("The Case for Larger Ground Forces"): "We live at a time when wars not only rage in nearly every region but threaten to erupt in many places where the current relative calm is tenuous. . . . No country besides the United States is in a position to lead the way in countering major challenges to the global order."

The army and marines want more troops. President George W. Bush wants them, too, as do many Democrats such as New York Sen. Hillary Clinton, Illinois Sen. Barack Obama, and New Mexico Gov. Bill Richardson. So does the Progressive Policy Institute and the Center for American Progress.

But before the United States assumes the role of global cop—with little need and great cost—it should think about what job it wants to give a larger ground force. Expanding the military without a clear strategy or mission puts the expansion cart well ahead of the strategic horse.

Set aside the real reason for the push to add more troops— the Iraq War. The war's long deployments, short at-home stays, and increased casualties are clearly stressing the army and the marines. But as Gen. George Casey Jr. put it recently, "The army I left in Iraq and the army I led there for two and a half years is hardly a broken army."

Virtually all defense analysts (in or out of uniform) concur that expanding the ground forces will not alleviate the current pressure on U.S. troops. Since it takes 3–5 years to produce a well-trained, deployable force, a larger ground force would only help in Iraq if we're still there around 2012.

Expanding the Military Is the Wrong Way to Counter Terrorism

So if a larger force won't help ease the current situation in Iraq, what strategy and mission will it assume? To the extent anyone has spoken or written about strategy, the justification seems to be "you never know." Casey says he wants his strategic reserve back as a hedge. Kagan and O'Hanlon worry about a disintegrating Pakistan, a collapsing Indonesia, a North Korean invasion of South Korea, or a nuclear-armed Iran. [In December 2006], the *Washington Post* wondered if we might need more forces to engage in a land conflict with China.

In a forthcoming piece in *The American Interest*, Lawrence Korb and Peter Ogden at the Center for American Progress make a slightly different argument: The United States needs more forces to engage in counterterrorism and counterinsurgency operations and to carry out stabilization and reconstruction missions in failed states. (Kagan and O'Hanlon also make this point.)

None of these justifications constitutes a strategy, and they all have severe problems. First, many depend on the notion that because we're stuck in Iraq, we can't do anything else without more troops. But once we leave Iraq, Casey will get his strategic reserve back.

Second, many of the future crisis scenarios are fantasies that no sensible policy maker will consider. The only reality-based argument for a larger combat force is the North Korean scenario. But we've deliberately encouraged the creation of a large, well-armed South Korean military to deter and counter such an invasion. Well before Iraq, we were reducing the visibility and size of the U.S. presence in South Korea. In fact, Army Gen. B. B. Bell, the commander in Korea, told the Senate Armed Services Committee in late April [2007], "It is doubtful that the North Korean military in its current state could sustain offensive operations against the South."

The Chinese and Indonesian scenarios are laughable. As for Iran, a ground invasion is unthinkable—the entire U.S. ground force would be unable to occupy, pacify, stabilize, and reconstruct a nation of 60 million people who don't want us there. Ninety-two thousand more troops won't change that. If

The War on Terrorism Will Not Be Won by Expanding the U.S. Military

If expanding the Army and Marines is all about the global war on terror, the United States could get a much greater payoff from investing $10 billion in building indigenous police, courts, schools, job-training centers, and health clinics—things that give Muslim populations reason to support their governments and reject the jihadists. But since Sept. 11, 2001, the resources that have gone into such important capabilities are a pittance compared with the increase in U.S. spending on military forces, most of which is irrelevant to this enemy.

To the extent that U.S. military capabilities need to be improved to counter terrorists, the investment should be in special operations forces and homeland defense, not land armies.

David C. Gompert, "No Need to Expand the U.S. Army,"
RAND Commentary, *January 26, 2007.*

we were foolish enough to preemptively strike Iran's nuclear capability, it would be by sea and/or air, only special forces would be on the ground.

The favorite scenario is Pakistan. A shaky regime, a strong current of Islamic fundamentalism, nuclear weapons—these are all elements of the nightmare scenario. But after any overthrow of the current Pakistani government, U.S. special forces (with the Pakistani military) would be tasked with securing Pakistan's warheads. Like Iran, a U.S. occupation opposed by 165 million angry Pakistanis would be impossible.

More Soldiers Can't Save Failed States

As for occupying, stabilizing, and reconstructing failed states and their economies, this mission (*not* a strategy) sounds a lot like "fighting the last war." We've conducted this mission for the past four years in Iraq (five in Afghanistan); more soldiers will not help us do it better. We might, as Korb and Ogden recommend, "train" U.S. soldiers for international and internal policing, nation-building, reconstruction, or even public diplomacy. That still doesn't change the fact that they're the wrong instrument for the job, and by doing it, they're dragged away from their core mission and capability.

Dealing with the global reality that states fail demands two things—neither of which have anything to do with expanding U.S. ground forces. First, it's critical to develop a multilateral approach to the problem, especially given that many parts of the world are uneasy about having the U.S. military involved in such missions. Second, we need to create national and international capabilities outside of the military—expertise in law enforcement, governance, and economic recovery—to aid in nation-building efforts. Expanding the U.S. ground force for this mission gains nothing.

As for counterinsurgency, one would think the United States would realize that history is littered with failed counterinsurgency operations, especially for Western military powers in countries where they are not welcome—i.e., Vietnam and Iraq. In Iraq, we're dealing with an insurgency *and* a civil war, making the task even more impossible. The army's new counterinsurgency manual (no matter the number of soldiers implementing it) is unlikely to reverse that history.

Finally, if the mission is counterterrorism, a larger army is not the right answer. Skilled special forces are more likely to be the uniformed instrument of choice. And success will depend on allied cooperation, policing, diplomacy, and tracking financial flows—activities that are not the military's responsibility.

Expansion Is Expensive

As for cost, expansion is expensive. The Congressional Budget Office estimates that adding the forces requested by President

Bush would require a minimum of $108 billion over the next five years; the army estimates $112 billion. We can afford it. The problem is that once the Defense Department leaves Iraq, the flood of emergency supplemental funding will end and defense budgets will likely shrink. At the same time, the Pentagon will have 92,000 more mouths to feed, train, and equip.

Lastly, it will be difficult and expensive to raise this force. To ensure it can meet its current goals, the army has lowered its recruiting standards in terms of educational experience, moral behavior, and age, and pushed recruitment spending to 20 times the pre-Iraq levels. So finding the recruits to fill out an enlarged military is going to be a real challenge.

The case for expanding the military then rests on a "hedge" against the unknown—creating a larger force without a clear strategic justification or mission. Post-Iraq, the existing force will serve as this "hedge." A larger force, however, might prove counterproductive to national security, as the long list of missions the United States could give a larger force sends the wrong message to the rest of the world—namely that the United States will continue to be the global constabulary and stabilizer of choice.

The U.S. presence in Iraq has already sent this message, and Washington has found that the rest of the world is no longer receptive to it. The future of our ability to lead internationally and the future role of military force in our statecraft depends on clearly defining strategy before we add personnel. And it will rest on a different style of global engagement, one that works with allies and uses all the tools of statecraft. Once home, our current forces are more than adequate to play their appropriate role in that broader strategy of engagement.

Periodical Bibliography

The following articles have been selected to supplement the diverse views presented in this chapter.

Central Committee for Conscientious Objectors
: "Should the All Volunteer Force Be Replaced by Universal Mandatory National Service" *Congressional Digest*, September 2006.

Deborah Davis
: "Illegal Immigrants: Uncle Sam Wants You," *In These Times*, July 25, 2007.

Philip Gold
: "Outside View: Alternatives to the Draft," *The Things You Do, America*, December 4, 2006, http://philipgold.wordpress.com/philips-articles/the-draft/alternatives-to-the-draft.

John Merrow
: "Army Recruiters: 'Counseling' High Schoolers to Death," *Education Digest*, February 2005.

Charles Moskos
: "Should the All Volunteer Force Be Replaced by Universal Mandatory National Service," *Congressional Digest*, September 2006.

David Morris
: "Issues and Allegations: Military Privatization," *American Voice*, 2004, www.newrules.org/voice2004/privatization/militarypriv.html.

H. David Pendleton
: "Saving the All-Volunteer Army," *Officer*, June 2005.

PR Newswire
: "U.S. Adults Do Not Support Draft for Military or Civilian Service, but Favor Voluntary Service to Support Country," February 23, 2007.

Matthew Quirk
: "Private Military Contractors," *Atlantic*, September 2004.

S. Douglas Smith and Bob Herbert
: "Should Military Recruiters Be Allowed in High Schools?" *New York Times Upfront*, March 13, 2006.

Josh White
: "Army's 'Quick Ship' Bonus Proves Popular," *WashingtonPost.com*, August 26, 2007, www.msnbc.msn.com/id/20453080.

For Further Discussion

Chapter 1

1. Walter L. Stewart Jr. bases his argument that the all-volunteer army is a failure on troop *quantity*: insufficient numbers stretched too thinly and falling recruitment. Bernard D. Rostker bases his argument that the all-volunteer army is a success on troop *quality*: better-educated recruits with higher socioeconomic status and higher intelligence scores. In your opinion, which is a better measure of the success or failure of the all-volunteer force? Which is a more persuasive argument for reinstating the draft? Explain your answers.

2. Phillip Carter, Paul Glastris, and Lawrence J. Korb disagree on the need for more troops in Iraq, but they agree that the kind of war the all-volunteer army is designed to fight—"a limited campaign for limited ends, of limited duration, and with a defined exit strategy"—is not the kind of war the United States is fighting in the twenty-first century. Using evidence presented in these authors' viewpoints, in your opinion, what kind of military force would be most effective in Iraq, and would conscripts or volunteers be more likely to produce such a force?

3. Julian E. Barnes and Peter Spiegel tally costs in terms of actual dollars spent on enlistment bonuses and recruitment initiatives for volunteers. John C. Goodman tallies costs in terms of theoretical dollars *not* earned and goods *not* produced by draftees who leave civilian life. In your view, are these calculations equally valid? Which do you find more persuasive in the debate over the costs of conscription versus the all-volunteer force? Explain your answer.

4. The army's enlistment agreement does not expressly describe a scenario in which a soldier's enlistment can be extended without his consent, but according to Daniel C. Brown it does state that Congress may "change or add to his obligations . . . regardless of the content of the enlistment agreement" and "it does not purport to list all circumstances under which a soldier's term of service may be extended." Enlistees must acknowledge that they have read and understood the agreement they are signing. Why then does Christopher Hayes call stop-loss orders a breach of the enlistment agreement? In your opinion, are the agreement's terms deceptive? If so, how should the agreement be clarified, and what obligation does the army have to ensure that enlistees really do understand its terms?

Chapter 2

1. Do you agree with David Greenberg that "without a just war, it is impossible to have a just draft." If so, why? If not, under what circumstances could a military draft be just though the war is unjust? Under what circumstances could a military draft be unjust though the war is just? Use examples from Greenberg's viewpoint to support your argument.

2. Both Michelle Cottle and Tim Kane use the military's own recruiting data to reach contradictory conclusions, Cottle that troop quality is declining, Kane that troop quality has not declined. How does their evidence differ, and whose evidence do you find more persuasive?

Chapter 3

1. Philip Gold and Erin Solaro present women's draft eligibility as a feminist issue. R. Cort Kirkwood objects to women's draft eligibility on religious and moral grounds. Based on evidence in the viewpoints, what restrictions if any do you believe should be placed on women's military service?

2. John Shalikashvili is a former chairman of the Joint Chiefs of Staff whose reversal of his opposition to openly gay men and women in the military coincides with the army's need to fill serious troop shortages. J. Matt Barber is policy director for a conservative Christian organization that condemns homosexuality as immoral. How does knowledge of their professional positions affect your assessment of their argument that openly gay servicepeople will (Barber) or will not (Shalikashvili) disrupt unit cohesion? Consider an aspect of the issue neither man addresses: If openly gay men and women are *not* eligible for the draft, how can the the military prevent people from evading the draft by claiming to be homosexual?

3. The Alliance for Security argues that a lottery is the fairest method of selecting draftees. Charles S. Abell suggests that a limited draft of people with critical specialized skills would be most effective and not unfair. Based on their arguments, if a draft becomes necessary, how do you think it should be conducted?

Chapter 4

1. William A. Galston calls universal military service a civic duty Americans should readily perform in exchange for the rights of citizenship they enjoy. Bruce Chapman limits civic duties to abiding by the law, serving on juries, unforced voting, voluntary community service, and military service only "if absolutely necessary." Based on your reading of their viewpoints, what do you believe are Americans' civic duties and how should they be discharged?

2. According to Michelle Gutiérrez, the U.S. government has turned to private contractors for supplies and services once provided by military personnel. Do you believe this is a good alternative to a military draft? If so, which supplies and services should and should not be provided by private contractors? If not, why not?

Organizations to Contact

The editors have compiled the following list of organizations concerned with the issues debated in this book. The descriptions are derived from materials provided by the organizations. All have publications or information available for interested readers. The list was compiled on the date of publication of the present volume; the information provided here may change. Be aware that many organizations take several weeks or longer to respond to inquiries, so allow as much time as possible.

American Friends Service Committee (AFSC)
1501 Cherry St., Philadelphia, PA   19102
(215) 241-7000 • fax: (215) 241-7275
e-mail: afscinfo@afsc.org
Web site: www.afsc.org

The AFSC is a Quaker organization committed to nonviolence and social justice. Founded in 1917 to give conscientious objectors opportunities to serve civilian war victims, the Nobel Prize–winning group opposes the draft and supports nonviolent resistance to international injustice. Its resources include brochures and leaflets such as *Draft Registration Options*; the counter-recruitment training manual *Before You Enlist and After You Say No*; reports on military service related to immigrants, gay and lesbian youth, and the poor; and CD-ROMs such as *Introduction to Youth and Militarism*.

AmeriCorps
1201 New York Ave. NW, Washington, DC   20525
(202) 606-5000 • fax: (202) 606-3472
e-mail: questions@americorps.org
Web site: www.americorps.org

A program established in 1994 through the federal Corporation for National & Community Service, AmeriCorps is a network of local, state, and national service programs in which some seventy thousand civic-minded Americans volunteer each year. In the debate over reinstatement of the military draft, advocates of compulsory universal national service often cite AmeriCorps as a model for a nonmilitary alternative to active-duty military service. The Web site offers catalogs of AmeriCorps programs as well as statistics on citizen participation, fact sheets, public service announcements, and a calendar of seminars and training activities designed to encourage citizen participation to strengthen community and country.

Center for Strategic and Budgetary Assessments (CSBA)
1667 K St. NW, Washington, DC   20006
(202) 331-7990 • fax: (202) 331-8019
e-mail: info@csbaonline.org
Web site: www.csbaonline.org

The center is a nonpartisan think tank that researches the present and future requirements, and present and future costs, of the U.S. national defense. It analyzes homeland security personnel needs, military preparedness in reports such as "The Future of U.S. Ground Forces: Challenges and Requirements," and the costs of military modernization and current military operations. Publications available at the Web site include strategic studies, defense budget studies, transcripts of congressional briefings, and recommendations for the transformation of the all-volunteer force.

Center on Conscience & War (CCW)
1830 Connecticut Ave. NW, Washington, DC   20009
(202) 483-2220
e-mail: webmaster@CenteronConscience.org
Web site: www.centeronsconscience.org

The center was founded in 1940 as the National Service Board for Religious Objectors, an association of groups representing conscientious objectors (COs) to World War II. Under its name since 2000, the nonprofit center continues to oppose all forms of conscription, defends the rights of both COs and active-duty military personnel, and develops constructive al-

ternatives to military service for people who refuse to participate in the event a military draft is reinstated. Its publications
include the quarterly newsletter *Reporter*; brochures and fact
sheets on draft law, registration, and conscientious objection;
and critical analyses of military enlistment programs.

G.I. Rights Hotline

405 14th St., Suite 205, Oakland, CA   94612
(800) 394-9544 • fax: (510) 465-2459
e-mail: girights@objector.org
Web site: www.objector.org/girights

A project of the Central Committee for Conscientious Objectors, based in Oakland and Philadelphia, the hotline is an-
swered by a coalition of nonprofit, nongovernmental antidraft
organizations that counsel and inform servicemembers about
military discharges, conscientious objection and other kinds of
draft resistance, grievance filings, and AWOL situations. Its
publications include the booklet *Helping Out: A Guide to Military Discharges and GI Rights* and advisories for COs in the
armed forces.

No Draft, No Way

55 W. 17th St., New York, NY   10011
(212) 633-6646
e-mail: info@NoDraftNoWay.org
Web site: www.NoDraftNoWay.org

No Draft, No Way is a grass-roots campaign initiated in 2004
by veterans, students, parents, and activists to oppose the possible return of the military draft and to challenge military recruiting practices. The organization publishes the book *We
Won't Go!*, antidraft petitions and posters, and the manual
Primer on Draft Resistance, available at the Web site along with
archives of Selective Service System documents and links to
other draft-related organizations.

Selective Service System (SSS)

National Headquarters, Arlington, VA   22209-2425
(703) 605-4100 • fax: (703) 605-4106
e-mail: information@sss.gov
Web site: www.sss.gov

The SSS is the federal agency responsible for supplying manpower to the armed forces in an emergency—it fulfills this mission in the early 2000s by registering all eligible males for the military draft and by its readiness to conduct a "timely, fair, and equitable" draft should one become necessary. The service's comprehensive Web site offers an archive of draft-related executive orders and legislation since the Vietnam War era, induction statistics, instructions for mandatory registration, and step-by-step explanation of the draft lottery. Publications available for download include annual reports to Congress, educational charts and brochures, and a quarterly newsletter, the *Register*.

U.S. Department of Defense: Defense Manpower Data Center (DMDC)

1600 Wilson Blvd., Suite 400, Arlington, VA   22209-2593
(703) 696-7398
e-mail: webmaster@osd.pentagon.mil
Web site: www.dmdc.osd.mil/dmdc.html

The DMDC is a comprehensive collection of personnel, manpower, training, and financial data in the Department of Defense. Among the information it compiles for the office of the Secretary of Defense is worldwide distribution of military personnel by year, geographical region, and service branch; troop strength; and casualties. It also lists military procurement records, i.e., what the armed services pay for supplies, equipment, and services from outside contractors, and identifies trends in military procurement. Its records are presented in easy electronic-browsing format, and offer useful insight into the distribution and activity of the all-volunteer armed forces.

U.S. Department of Defense Personnel and Readiness (P&R) Office
4000 Defense Pentagon, Washington, DC   20301-4000
(703) 695-0105 • fax: (703) 571-9338
Web site: www.defenselink.mil/prhome

Of interest to student researchers, the P&R office manages the national ROTC and other military college programs and sponsors the My Future Program, a site for students that describes military careers, skills assessment, and post–high school military job options in the all-volunteer army. Publications available at the Web site include the *Personnel and Readiness 2006–2011 Strategic Plan*; reports on military pay and benefits, recruiting policy, and the reorganization of all-volunteer active-duty forces; and updated news articles about the mobilization and training of the reserve forces.

War Resisters League (WRL)
339 Lafayette St., New York, NY   10012
(212) 228-0450 • fax: (212) 228-6193
e-mail: wrl@warresisters.org
Web site: www.warresisters.org

Founded in 1923, the league is an independent, nonpartisan pacifist organization that opposes conscription in the belief that all war, international or civil, is a crime against humanity and advocates Gandhian nonviolent action to resolve conflict and achieve social change. The league's Youth and Counter-militarism Program works to limit military-recruiting activity in the schools and give students opportunities to interact with returning soldiers from their communities who want to speak out against war. Numerous resources include the organizing manual *DMZ: A Guide to Taking Your School Back from the Military*; antidraft and anti-enlistment brochures, flyers, and fact sheets; the quarterly magazine *WIN*; and links to other antidraft organizations and the league's international affiliate, War Resisters International.

Bibliography of Books

Aimee Allison
and David Solnit

Army of None. New York: Seven Stories, 2007.

Beth Asch

Looking to the Future: What Does Transformation Mean for Military Manpower and Personnel Policy? Santa Monica, CA: RAND, 2004.

David Axe

Army 101: Inside ROTC in a Time of War. Columbia: University of South Carolina Press, 2007.

Andrew J.
Bacevich

The New American Militarism: How Americans Are Seduced by War. New York: Oxford University Press, 2005.

Aaron Belkin
and Geoffrey
Bateman, eds.

Don't Ask, Don't Tell: Debating the Gay Ban in the Military. Boulder, CO: Lynne Rienner, 2003.

Peter Brock

Against the Draft: Essays on Conscientious Objection from the Radical Reformation to the Second World War. Toronto, ONT: University of Toronto Press, 2006.

Kingsley Browne

Co-Ed Combat: The New Evidence that Women Shouldn't Fight the Nation's Wars. New York: Sentinel HC, 2007.

E.J. Dionne Jr.,
Kayla Meltzer
Drogosz, and
Robert E. Litan,
eds.

United We Serve: National Service and the Future of Citizenship. Washington, DC: Brookings Institution Press, 2003.

Tod Ensign | *America's Military Today: Challenges for the Armed Forces in a Time of War*. New York: New Press, 2006.

Michael S. Foley | *Confronting the War Machine: Draft Resistance During the Vietnam War*. Chapel Hill: University of North Carolina Press, 2007.

Curtis L. Gilroy, Barbara A. Bicksler, and John T. Warner | *The All-Volunteer Force: Thirty Years of Service*. Dulles, VA: Potomac, 2004.

Curtis Gilroy and Cindy Williams, eds. | *Service to Country: Personnel Policy and the Transformation of Western Militaries*. Cambridge, MA: MIT Press, 2007.

Philip Gold | *The Coming Draft: The Crisis in Our Military and Why Selective Service Is Wrong for America*. New York: Presidio, 2006.

Stephanie Gutmann | *The Kinder, Gentler Military: How Political Correctness Affects Our Ability to Win Wars*. New York: Encounter, 2001.

Samuel P. Huntington | *The Soldier and the State: The Theory and Politics of Civil-Military Relations*. 1957. Rev. ed. Cambridge, MA: Harvard University Press, Belknap, 2005.

Chalmers Johnson | *The Sorrows of Empire: Militarism, Secrecy, and the End of the Republic*. New York: Owl, 2004.

Peter Karsten, ed.   *Recruiting, Drafting, and Enlisting: Two Sides of the Raising of Military Forces.* 5 vols. London: Routledge, 1998.

Ronald R. Krebs   *Fighting for Rights: Military Service and the Politics of Citizenship.* Ithaca, NY: Cornell University Press, 2006.

Thomas S. Langston   *Uneasy Balance: Civil-Military Relations in Peacetime America Since 1783.* Baltimore, MD: Johns Hopkins University Press, 2003.

Anne S. Mavor   *Assessing Fitness for Military Enlistment: Physical, Medical, and Mental Health Standards.* National Research Council. Washington, DC: National Academy Press, 2006.

Lars Mjoset and Stephen Van Holde, eds.   *The Comparative Study of Conscription in the Armed Forces.* Oxford: Elsevier Science, 2002.

Daniel Moran and Arthur Waldron, eds.   *The People in Arms: Military Myth and National Mobilization Since the French Revolution.* Cambridge, U.K.: Cambridge University Press, 2002.

Bernard Rostker   *I Want You! The Evolution of the All-Volunteer Force.* Santa Monica, CA: RAND, 2006.

Kathy Roth-Douquet and Frank Schaeffer   *AWOL: The Unexcused Absence of America's Upper Classes from Military Service—and How It Hurts Our Country.* New York: Collins, 2006.

Sam C. Sarkesian
and Robert E.
Connor Jr.
The U.S. Military Profession into the Twenty-First Century: War, Peace, and Politics. 2nd ed. London: Routledge, 2006.

Jeremy Scahill
Blackwater: The Rise of the World's Most Powerful Mercenary Army. New York: Nation, 2007.

P.W. Singer
Corporate Warriors: The Rise of the Privatized Military Industry. Ithaca, NY: Cornell University Press, 2003.

Erin Solaro
Women in the Line of Fire: What You Should Know About Women in the Military. Toronto: Seal, 2006.

James Tracy, ed.
The Military Draft Handbook: A Brief History and Practical Advice for the Curious and Concerned. San Francisco: Manic D. Press, 2005.

Index

A

Abell, Charles S., 160
Abizaud, John, 54
Adams, Gordon, 212
Agricultural establishment, 78
Alliance for Security, 153
All-volunteer military
  can supply enough troops,
    53–62
  draft is cheaper than, 63–69
  draft is more costly than,
    70–78
  evolution of, 34–35
  failure of, 22–31
  inequality in, 179–182
  is a success, 32–41
  is not supplying enough
    troops, 42–52
  problems with, 128, 172–174
  ROTC program and, 195–199
  universal service should re-
    place, 170–183
Alvarez, Lizette, 112
American Revolution, conscription
  during, 15, 104
AmeriCorps, 174, 182, 187
Antidraft protests
  during Civil War, 15
  during Vietnam War, 16–17,
    35, 96
Antiwar demonstrations
  against Iraq War, 96–97
  during Vietnam War, 16–17,
    96
  during WWII, 16
Army suicides, 19
Asch, Beth, 38
Aspin, Les, 139

B

Backdoor draft, stop-loss policy is,
  79–85
Barber, J. Matt, 148
Barnes, Julian E., 63
Basic training
  gender normed, 137–138
  soldiers failing, 58–59
Bayh, Evan, 198
Bell, B.B., 215
Bender, Bryan, 200
Blackwater USA, 167, 168–169
Boot, Max, 206
Bosnia, 50
Brown, Daniel C., 86
Brown, John S., 16
Buckley, W. F., 197
Bush, George W., 64, 66, 144, 202,
  214

C

Callaghan, James, 29
Carafano, James Jay, 97
Carter, Hodding, 98
Carter, Jimmy, 155
Carter, Phillip, 42
Casey, George, Jr., 214, 215
Chapman, Bruce, 176, 184
Citizenship, 173–174, 177
Civic self-respect, 177–178
Civil War
  conscription during, 15, 105–
    106, 179
  recruitment during, 179, 206
Clinton, Bill, 139
Clinton, Hillary, 214

Cold War, 16, 106–107, 155, 213

Combat restrictions, on women, 131–133, 136–141

Commission on an All-Volunteer Armed Force, 25–27

Compulsory service. *See* Universal national service

Confederate Army, 15

Conscientious objector (CO) status, 15, 125

Conscription. *See* Draft

Continental Army, 15, 104

Corporation for National and Community Service, 174

Costs
    of draft, 70–78
    of military expansion, 217–218
    opportunity, 71–73
    of universal service, 190, 191–193

Cottle, Michelle, 109

Counterinsurgents, 217

Counterinsurgency operations, 60

D

Dancs, Anita, 65

Decline and Fall of the Roman Empire (Gibbon), 23

Defense budget, 39

Defense industries, 78

Deferments, 78, 125–126

Desert Storm, 50

Desertions, 19

Donnelly, Elaine, 150

"Don't ask, don't tell" policy, 61, 143–147

Draft
    benefits of, 66–69, 100
    constitutionality of, 129

    costs more than all-volunteer military, 70–78
    does not need to be reinstated, 32–41
    evaluation of, 74–77
    historical use of, 14–17, 104–107, 154–155
    is cheaper than all-volunteer military, 63–69
    opposition to, 76–77, 105
    political economy of, 77–78
    should be reinstated, 19, 21–31, 42–52
    stop-loss policy is back-door, 79–85
    three-tiered, 27
    during Vietnam War, 125–126
    women should be eligible for, 127–133
    women should not be eligible for, 134–142
    would divide society, 102–108
    would improve troop quality, 109–114
    would not improve troop quality, 115–122
    would unify society, 98–101

Draft evaders, 125

Draft process, 157–159

Draft registration
    during Cold War, 16
    reinstatement of, in 1980, 17, 155

Draft resistors
    during Civil War, 15
    during Vietnam War, 16–17

Draft-card burning, 17

Draftees
    should be selected based on skills, 160–164
    should be selected by lottery, 153–159

DREAM Act, 204

E

Economic effects, of draft, 70–78
Education levels, of recruits, 36, 111–113, 118–121
Eisenhower, Dwight, 77
Englin, David L., 178
Equipment shortages, 19–20, 48
Ethnicity, 36–37

F

Failed states, 216017
Female soldiers
    combat restrictions on, 61–62, 131–133
    See also Women
Fleming, Tom, 141
Foreign nationals, 203–205
Foreign recruitment, 200–206
Friedman, Milton, 24

G

Galston, William, 170
Gates, Robert M., 202
Gates, Tom, 25
Gay soldiers
    "don't ask, don't tell" policy and, 61, 143–147
    should be openly accepted in military, 143–147
    should not be accepted in military, 148–152
Gear shortages, 19–20, 48
Gender, 36
Geographic representation, of recruits, 37
GI Bill, 176
Gibbon, Edward, 23
Glastris, Paul, 42
Goff, Stan, 83
Gold, Philip, 127, 187

Goldfarb, Ronald, 98
Gombert, David C., 216
Goodman, Ellen, 130
Goodman, John C., 70
Government, nature of, 23
Greenberg, David, 102
Greenewalt, Crawford, 39–40
Greenspan, Alan, 24
Greenya, John, 190
Ground forces, expansion of, 59–62, 66
Gutiérrez, Michelle, 207

H

Hart, Pamela, 81, 83
Hasbrouck, Edward, 96
Hayes, Christopher, 79
Helmly, James, 47
Hershey, Lewis B., 107
Hesburgh, Theodore M., 24–25
Hess, Stephen, 181
Homeland security, 50–51, 185
Homosexuality, 126
Homosexuals
    "don't ask, don't tell" policy and, 61, 143–147
    should be openly accepted in military, 143–147
    should not be accepted in military, 148–152

I

Immigrants, 201–203, 204
In re Grimley, 90–91
Incentive bonuses, 113–114
Individual Ready Reserve (IRR), 79–85
Iraq War
    demonstrations against, 96–97
    enlistment decline during, 40

equipment shortages in, 48
misuse of troops during, 53–62
strains on U.S. Army caused by, 19–20, 57–59
troops needed for, 44–48, 214–215

J

Johnson, Lyndon, 107
Johnson, Shoshana, 141
Jury duty, 176–177

K

Kagan, Frederick, 214, 215
Kane, Tim, 115
Kerry, John, 87
Kirkwood, R. Cort, 134
Korb, Lawrence J., 53, 215
Korean War, 16, 49, 155, 180
Kosovo, 50
Kurtz, Stanley, 195
Kuwait, 49

L

Legal residents, 201–203
Liberties, 76–77
Lincoln, Abraham, 14, 179
Litan, Robert, 176, 186, 187, 192
Lottery system, 17, 153–159
Lynch, Jessica, 140

M

Madison, James, 104
Mandatory military service. *See* Conscription
Mandatory Service Obligation (MDO), 81
Mariscal, Jorge, 204
Marital status, 36

McCain, John, 87, 101, 198
McPherson, James, 179
Mental aptitude, 36
Mercenaries, 168
    See also Private military contractors
Military contracts, 168
Military enlistment, obligations of, 86–93
Military expansion, U.S. should not pursue, 212–218
Military officers, 78
Military preparedness, 73–74
Military recruitment
    during Civil War, 179
    costs of, 64–66, 68–69
    difficulties of, 22, 68
    failure of, 57–59
    of foreigners, 200–206
    Iraq War and, 40
    opening of, 61–62
    standards for, 65–66
    targeted programs for, 39
    volunteer, can supply enough troops, 53–62
    volunteer, is not supplying enough troops, 42–52
Military training, women and, 137–138
Militias, 129–131
Mill, John Stuart, 175
Monroe, James, 104
Moore, Michael, 116
Morality
    of universal service, 188–189
    of women in combat, 138–140
Moskos, Charles, 27, 68

N

National and Community Service Act, 187
National Guard, calling up of, for Iraq War, 47

Nicholson, Jim, 67

Niskanen, William, 193

Nixon, Richard, 24–25, 35, 107, 155

No-bid contracts, 168

North Korea, 215

O

Obama, Barack, 214

Ogden, Peter, 215

O'Hanlon, Michael, 204–205, 214, 215

O'Meara, Kevin, 82, 84

On Liberty (Mill), 175

Opportunity costs, 71–73

Optional citizenship, 173

P

Pacifists, during WWII, 16

Pakistan, 216

Patriotism, 99–100

Peacekeeping missions, 60

Pelosi, Nancy, 149

Persian Gulf War, 49, 50

Political economy, of draft, 77–78

President, power of, to extend enlistments, 88–89

Prince, Erik, 167

Prisoners of war (POW), female, 140–141

Private military contractors

    advantages of, 167–168

    disadvantages of, 168

    hiring of, by U.S. military, 207–211

    numbers of, 167

    risks of, 210–211

Privatized military industry (PMI), 208–211

Q

Quantitative analysis, 38–39

Quindlen, Anna, 105

R

Race, 36–37

Randolph, Edmund, 104

Rangel, Charles B., 66–67, 97, 103, 107–108, 196

Ratner, Michael, 168

Ray, Ron, 138–139

Recruitment. *See* Military recruitment

Recruits

    with criminal backgrounds, 112

    draft would improve quality of, 109–114

    draft would not improve quality of, 115–122

    education levels of, 36, 111–113, 118–121

    incentive bonuses for, 113–114

    with medical problems, 112

    quality of, 65–66

    standards for wartime, 117–118

    waivers given to, 66

    without high school diplomas, 111–113

Reed, Jack, 68, 69

Regan, Tom, 48

Reservists, returning to active duty, 79–85

Resistance, to the draft, 15–17, 35, 96

Retention, 58

Richardson, Bill, 214

Ripley, John, 139

Roosevelt, Franklin, 106, 155

Rostker, Bernard D., 32, 65

ROTC (Reserve Officer Training Corps) programs, 195–199
Rumsfeld, Donald, 44, 82, 167

S

Satin, Mark, 67
Scahill, Jeremy, 167
Schaeffer, Frank, 198
Schoomaker, Peter, 88
Schwartz, Michael, 209
Selective Service Act (1917), 15
Selective Service Act (1950), 16, 161
Selective Service Agency, 17
Selective Service System (SSS)
    establishment of, 154, 155
    universal service should replace, 170–183
    during Vietnam War, 125
Shalikashvili, John M., 61, 143, 150, 151
Shapiro, Alan, 125
Shinseki, Eric, 44
Shortages
    of gear and weapons, 19–20, 48
    of troops, 42–52
Skelton, Ika, 203
Skills-based draft, 160–164
Socioeconomic status, 37
Solaro, Erin, 127
Soldiers. See Troops
Spectator citizenship, 173–174
Spiegel, Peter, 63
State militias, 129–131
States, failed, 216017
Stewart, Walter L. Jr., 19, 21
Stop-loss policy
    is "back-door" draft, 79–85
    is legal extension of voluntary enlistment, 86–93

Stroup, Theodore G., 64
Suicides, among soldiers, 19

T

Terrorism, 214–216, 217
Thompson, Mark, 19, 19–20
Thurman, Maxwell, 37–38
Troop deployments, 19
Troops
    current strains on, 19–20, 57–59
    demographics of, 36–37, 121–122
    draft would improve quality of, 109–114
    draft would not improve quality of, 115–122
    extending tours of duty of, 79–85
    female, 61–62, 131–133
    gay, 61, 143–152
    misuse of, in Iraq War, 53–62
    needed for Iraq War, 44–48
    quality of, 65–66, 117–118
    shortage of, 42–52
    test scores of, 38–39
    See also Recruits
Trotter, Paul, 81–82, 84
Truman, Harry, 106–107
Tyson, Ann Scott, 90

U

United States
    does not need to reinstate draft, 32–41
    should not pursue military expansion, 212–218
    should reinstate draft, 21–31
Universal Militia Act (1972), 129
Universal national service
    as better option, 129

costs of, 190, 191–193

is bad idea, 184–194

should replace selective service, 170–183

unintended consequences of, 189–191

U.S. Army, expansion of, 59–62, 66

U.S. Marine, expansion of, 59–62, 66

U.S. military

current strains on, 19–20, 42–52, 57–59

equipment shortages in, 19–20, 48

failure of all-volunteer, 22–31

homosexuals should be accepted in, 61, 143–147

homosexuals should not be accepted in, 148–152

overstaffing in, 56

retention in, 58

social representation in, 36–37

standards for, 59, 118–121

success of all-volunteer, 32–41

use of private contractors by, 207–211

women in, 61–62, 131–133

U.S. society

draft would divide, 102–108

draft would unify, 98–101

V

Vandenberg, Arthur, 106

Vietnam War

antidraft protests during, 16–17, 35, 96

deferments during, 125–126

draft during, 125–126

number of soldiers in, 49

VISTA, 187

W

War of 1812, 104

War on terrorism, 214–216, 217

War protesters. *See* Antiwar demonstrations

Washington, George, 104

Weapons shortages, 19–20

Weinberger, Caspar W., 28

Westmoreland, William, 107

White, Thomas, 44

Williams, Armstrong, 100

Williams, Cindy, 56

Williams, Walter, 75

Wilson, Woodrow, 106

Women

combat restrictions on, 131–133, 136–141

lack of physical prowess in, 136–137

should be eligible for draft, 127–133

should not be eligible for draft, 134–142

soldiers, 61–62

World War I, conscription during, 15, 105–106

World War II

conscription during, 15–16, 106, 154–155

military service during, 180